IMPACT OF A DELIVERANCE PRAYER
A STUDY OF DELIVERANCE MINISTRY

By Dr. Ernest Maddox

Published By Dr. Ernest Maddox,   Third Edition, June 2013
Unauthorized Duplication Prohibited

P.O. Box 48547, Oak Park, MI. 48237 Phone 248 -796-8523

Email drddox@yahoo.com www.dremaddox.org

ISBN 978-0-9779748-2-5

Table of Contents

Acknowledgments

God
Jesus
Holy Spirit
Wife Barbara
Mother Gertha
Colleague Group
Family and Friends
Apostle Fred Harris
Dissertation Committee
Study Observation Team
Church of the Risen Christ
Ecumenical Theological Seminary
POINTE of Light Christian Center

The Sword
Of The
Spirit
Which
Is The
Word of God

And Many Others To Numerous To Name
I THANK ALL OF YOU FOR A SOLID FOUNDATION!

Abstract

This was an event to observe the supernatural, theoretically provoked by a specific format of Deliverance Prayer. The purpose of this treatise/study was to ascertain, whether or not a specific format of Deliverance Prayer would cause impact in the form of reaction(s), and or behavior(s) on the lives of individuals seeking deliverance. The study did establish that impact occurred in the form of a set of reaction(s), and, behavior(s). Some areas of history, controversy and interpretation from different authors and practitioners, including myself, relative to deliverance/spiritual warfare ministry, had to be and were reviewed. Four of the ten study participants were interviewed four months later relative to the impact on their lives; based on their feedback impact did and has continued to occur. The vehicles for this endeavor included: the Journey, Theory/Literature Review, Methodology, Ministry Research Event, Post Ministry Research Event Data Review, Post Ministry Event - Impact Evaluation Interviews, Reflection and Study Process Impact chapters, of this study. Appendixes A through F present study data result categories, some definitions of terms used in this study, and selected reference reviews.

Question

Will a specific format of deliverance prayer impact the lives of people in need of deliverance?

Goals

The goals are to ascertain whether or not impact in the form of reaction(s) and behavior(s) will occur as a result of a specific Deliverance Prayer, and annotate the types and nature of the reaction(s) and behavior(s) of the individuals prayed for:

Categorize each impact based on the type of reaction(s) and behavior(s) that manifest during the prayer.

Respond to the question using the data collected during the study process.

Informal Hypothesis/Theory

At this point in my journey I have two informal theories/hypotheses relative to deliverance:

There will be some recognizable impact in the form of reaction(s) and behavior(s) to a specific format of Deliverance Prayer.

Deliverance prayer and deliverance activity impacts the supernatural world of evil spirits, as well as good spirits.

Another purpose of this treatise is to some degree address informal theory/hypothesis number one. Informal theory/hypothesis number two will not be directly addressed in this treatise/study.

Forward

The nature of this ministry research event requires some introductory remarks. My intent with the question was to keep the area of study as focused as possible. The inherent challenges of attempting to put a supernatural phenomenon into some kind of informal/formal format can be insurmountable. I purposely focused on the practitioner's perspective with authors who are practitioners. This process did not exclude nor is it void of academic input, such as psychological and social science influences. This was not intended to be a pure scientific research project. It was intended to be a ministry event experience motivated by a journey, born out of one event relative to a specific format of Deliverance Prayer impact.

The Theory/Literature Review chapter reflects my intent to keep the scope focused and at the same time identify some well-known, and not so well-known authors and practitioners. I endeavored to present some areas of controversy that still exists today while staying focused on some of the areas that I suspected would surface as impact, in the form of reaction(s) and behavior(s), during the ministry research event.

The Theory/Literature Review chapter also provides some history relative to deliverance ministry along with some of the controversies. I did not endeavor to address all of the deliverance ministry controversies in this study, nor did I attempt to address every argument connected to the controversies I broached.

The methodological approach also was designed to keep the process focused. My intent was to determine and document whether impact would occur in the form of reaction(s), and behaviors(s), and to present the outcomes in a way that would provide a basic understanding. This was not intended to be a pure qualitative or quantitative process, but a combination of both processes that could bring some understanding to what may be considered supernatural activity.

Flexibility of data presentation, was another consideration relative to the selected approach. This process did manifest limitations and challenges that has and will raise questions that could be areas of research. What is ultimately important is that the question of this thesis was answered through this process.

Peripheral issues had to be broached for background, history, theory, and methodology considerations. I did not attempt to be exhaustive by design relative to the peripheral issues; to do so would have extended this study beyond its scope. To respond in detail to every question, concern, scriptural, theological, and denominational issue raised during this process was not feasible nor the purpose. As an engaged practitioner, I embarked upon this process with a preference for immediate results. More than anything else it was intended to be a ministry event, with immediate observable result(s), and impact, in the form of reaction(s) and behavior(s).

One of several areas of potential debate will be my reference to a cosmic conflict or cosmic rebellion, as a pre-Adam and Eve event. Some may consider this speculative and risky, but the premise does have some Biblical support. I stand by the cosmic conflict statement. If a debate and research are stimulated relative to where and how spiritual warfare originated, then let the research and debate begin.

I believe that Satan and the demons exist and that a pre-Adam and Eve event took place as described in Isaiah 14 and Ezekiel 28. Jesus Christ saw Satan fall from Heaven, Luke 10:18; there may be a great deal of debate about where and when, but not if. This perspective is important, and it is not an isolated one.

Other potential study related questions could emerge from dialogue related to mental illness verses demonization, variables relative to the observation process, and the absence of a comparative prayer process. These areas could become excellent study research topics. Are these limitations or process manifested opportunities?

All of the limitations and restrictions of this study were not design generated. Some limitations of this study are a result of the elusive nature of the supernatural. Other limitations will be based on perceptions of individuals, institutions, and theological articulations, which are beyond the control and scope of this study.

Areas of study that probe into the religious supernaturalism, or areas where man may not control, may cause a negative response to the one who is doing the probing. I am reminded of Wilson Brian Key's statement in *Subliminal Seduction*:

This view of man as being dominated by a mechanism within his mind of which he has no conscious knowledge is to many a frightening attack upon the ego. Anyone who incautiously probes into unconscious perceptions or motives may wind up ridiculed by an outraged, self-righteous mob. ... (Key, 1973, p. 47)

I acknowledge and accept the challenges of this study. But, I also encourage those who will be stimulated and inspired by this study to probe deeper into the questions, issues and concerns that emerged from this process. I know that this study will help some troubled souls, and inspire some to future research into the area of inner healing and deliverance ministry/spiritual warfare related prayer. I also acknowledge that my pro deliverance practitioner mindset may conflict with the liturgy of others.

Chapter One - Introduction
Chronological Overview-Spiritual Autobiography

I will briefly outline the events from 1969 unto the present. I received the Lord Jesus Christ and was baptized the summer of 1969. In 1976, I became a youth minister and began to coordinate, develop/design, and facilitate spiritual programs for youth ages six through eighteen. I developed and copyrighted programs that I utilized to train youth facilitators. I coordinated sports, educational, cultural, community out-reach and in-reach programs for youth involvement. These responsibilities and activities were executed for my home church, (I will use the term "my home church" when referring to the church I attended) and other churches or organizations that requested my assistance. The use of the term "my home church" to identify my church, is necessary in my opinion for anonymity. These experiences instilled commitment and endurance, as well as enhanced my spiritual growth.

I was ordained a deacon by my home church and was allowed to preach and teach the word of God to youth and adults through sermons. I produced a spiritual radio broadcast from 1998 to 2001. This broadcast was a continuation of my mission to share what God the Father and Jesus Christ had revealed to me. The broadcast was committed to connecting youth and adults to the word and the power of God (II Timothy 1:7), as well as dialogue about spiritual warfare.

"For God has not given us a spirit of fear, but of power and of love and of a sound mind" (II Timothy 1:7, New King James, NKJ). This continues to be the core of my ministry and journey.

I was licensed to preach the Gospel of Jesus Christ, by men outside of my home church, a validation of ordained men, for what God the Father had/has called and anointed me to do, an opportunity to serve in a broader arena.

I was ordained an Elder, by men outside of my home church, a recognition of the fruits of a dynamic ministry in the Father, Son, and Holy Spirit. There also was a realization in my life of the need for increased Bible study, prayer, and fasting to stay close to God. In August 1999, I entered the Ecumenical Theologian Seminary Doctorate of Ministry Program, to broaden my spiritual education and spiritual journey.

In April of 2000, I founded and became Pastor of The POINTE (People Organized In New Testament Empowerment) of Light Christian Center. Part of the mission is to conduct leadership and outreach training to all that have a desire to promote the Gospel of Jesus Christ, the Kingdom of God and serve in the community. The focus is development through training that addresses spiritual and physical needs, in addition to, preaching the Gospel and providing spiritual guidance to all. For me, deliverance ministry/spiritual warfare is and will remain the overall focus and purpose.

> The Spirit of the Lord is upon me, because he hath anointed me to preach the gospel to the poor; he hath sent me to heal the brokenhearted, to preach deliverance to the captives, and recovering of sight to the blind, to set at liberty them that are bruised, To preach the acceptable year of the Lord. (Luke 4:18-19 King James Version, KJV)

The importance of this text to this treatise will become obvious as we move forward in this process.

Physical Context

I spent almost thirty-one years as a member of my conservative home church, and I became a spiritual survivor of that process. There are many things that could be said about my experience as an African-American member of my home church, from 1969 until 2000, when I left to become a pastor. The experiences only helped to make me a more resolute Christian knowing that indeed there is a God. For that, I owe a debt of thanks to God the Father, Jesus Christ, the powerful/loving/sound minded producing Holy Spirit and my home church. However, I will outline some concerns I felt impeded my personal growth and my home church's growth. The major concerns I had/have are:

Racism

This impeded my personal growth, based on my experiences, from the perspective you had to be a passive African-American male to be accepted or recognized as a valuable leader. I was and am an aggressive and progressive African-American male. I was not allowed to develop or grow in the same way as less gifted and/or talented white males in my home church. The organization was racist and believed that God would have it that way. This attitude robbed, in my opinion, the organization of great potential in the way of human resources.

Bill Wylie-Kellerman sees racism as a principality

Racism is more than expression of an individual attitude; it is prejudice with power behind it. But looked upon with a biblical and theological eye, white racism may be recognized to be even more – an active and aggressive principality, a 'power' that appears to move, adapt, and grow with a life of its own. (Wylie-Kellerman, 1998, p. 9)

Music

The music was Eurocentric in nature and so called "African-American Gospel" or ethnic originated music was seen as less than the "The Will of God." Being a part of this organization was a culturally bankrupt experience relative to diversity in music.

Worship Forms

The services were very conservative, Puritan, unemotional, and dry. The attitude was that this is the only way God should be worshipped. Basically, congregational appeasement was the order of the day relative to music.

Fear of Another Culture

At one point, in certain areas of the country, blacks and whites could not sit in the same seating sections at services; even on church grounds at holy convocations. Blacks and whites could not intermarry;

the color of skin was always important. My home church operated under the premise that certain whites were considered descendants of the Israelites and all others, especially blacks were considered second class or gentiles. Anything non-white was considered by most leadership and laity as ungodly or evil.

Political Correctness

The political climate was whatever kept the majority white population of the church happy and tithing, was "The Will of God."

Man Worship

What men wanted was more important than what God wanted for far too many in leadership. Popularity was more important than obeying the word of God.

Religious/Spiritual Apartheid

Most members of the organization were treated based on race; at one point, if you were not white you could not attend my home church's colleges. Later that was relaxed to allow married blacks to attend. Finally much later, single blacks were allowed to attend. It should be understood that blacks paid tithes and offerings to support the colleges neither they nor their children could attend.

Powerful Deliverance Prayer

Prayer for the most part was weak and manifested very little power in many cases relative to the congregations I was involved with. Those who were in need of powerful deliverance prayer did not receive it.

These are some of the areas I felt had an emotional impact on me and kept the people polarized, and the leaders off center. It seemed that popularity was more important than what was right according to the Word of God.

Research regarding areas listed above relative to my home church would support what I have briefly stated; most if not all of this information is a matter of public record.

Spiritual Context

It is my intent to be brief in this area, because I want the focus of this treatise to stay on the question. The emotions that I experienced (bitterness, hate and rejection) as I journeyed through the process of my home church forced me to into a deeper prayer life, and set the stage for my attitude about prayer and deliverance for myself and those we call the churched population. The church that I have called and will always call my home church has changed in recent years and is now more sensitive to the Holy Spirit and the non-European /non-white cultures.

These experiences did open some wounds that needed to be healed. These experiences also exposed me to emotions that lead to the need for deliverance. Having professional working experience as a community mental health worker with a full caseload provided background to understand my conflict from a psychological perspective. One could say, "Why did you stay in that situation so long?" My response is, "I did not feel God had released me until March of 2000, when I felt that God said it was time to leave." I left with the blessings of my home church district leadership; it was not a hostile transition. I believe this was an ordained part of my journey to give birth to this treatise/study and the rest of my spiritual journey.

I have, by the Grace of God, been involved in outreach with other churches for over twenty years, and in professional/personal community outreach for over twenty-six years, while simultaneously providing youth and adult leadership within my home church. The experience of learning from, working in and collaborating with multi-cultural environments has earned me a reputation, on a national level, as one who can bring opposing factions together to reconcile and collaborate, both in the religious and secular arenas. One of the negative things that I have had to come to grips with is that most church organizations that claim multi-cultural composition are really practicing a form of religious/spiritual apartheid. In other words, we may be in this situation together, but we are not together in the situation. The group who has control and power will minimize and marginalize the rights of those who do not control or hold power.

I know, in the core of my being, that God has anointed me to serve, bringing to bear all of the skills and talents He has given to me. I understand the dynamics of racism, political correctness, religious/spiritual apartheid, congregational appeasement and the syndrome of popularity. I have seen what those dynamics have done to the leadership and members of the church that I call my home church for almost thirty-one years, as well as other church organizations, and I understand the residue that remains. Some of the residue is division, oppression, marginalization and demon infiltration. I realize that some Christians do not believe in the Devil or demons, and have a problem with Deliverance Ministry; my home church did. Some that were pastors and laity in my home church behaved in ways that appeared to others and myself, as individuals who needed deliverance from demons. These empirical beliefs and observations, are my expressions and perceptions of what I experienced.

One of the things that has been of interest to me in my journey as a Christian and minister, is how people are impacted by Deliverance Prayer. I was a part of a very conservative organization for almost thirty-one years, where prayer was very private, quiet and dignified. When people were prayed for relative to healing I saw very little or no impact at all. The ones I had an opportunity to ask indicated they basically felt nothing. Deliverance was not a stated part of theology for my home church. After a few years in this organization I began to explore other denominational prayer practices, and how people were impacted by prayer. What I have discovered is that the range is from quiet conservative to loud and highly animated.

I could not understand why people reacted in certain ways to a particular prayer style. I have been involved in what has been called Healing and Deliverance Prayer for more than twenty-five years. In the last three years I have focused in on what has been called deliverance prayer or "Prayer of Deliverance." I have been exposed to many types of what is called "Deliverance Prayers" that focused on healing and deliverance, and I have become curious as to why some seem to be more effective than others are.

Fifteen months before the study I had been involved with a Friday night inner healing and deliverance service. I recognize the wide range of variables relative to Deliverance Prayer, such as one's relationship with God, level of experience in the deliverance process, mindset, mental condition, and denominational borders/boundaries; and my curiosity still remains active. I believe that people need deliverance from evil spirits and Deliverance Prayer is a powerful tool. I have had direct confrontations with many demons over the last thirty plus years. Prayer and obedience to God is the only way to stop demons, based on my experience.

As I think about this process and the historical struggle I have had with the evil supernatural, I could have seen more victories along the way. When I consider the information compiled and how that information confirmed so much of my spiritual warfare battlefield empirical knowledge and understanding, I consider myself blessed.

The Theory/Literature Review chapter, which includes a dialogical and thematic review of selected literature, helped me to understand the historical resentments relative to deliverance ministry and the whole concept of spiritual warfare. I am able to understand, on a deeper level, the fear that lashed out in hate when I would ask questions about demons and demonic activity in the Church, Christian and religious environments. The basic response was/is, "Christians cannot have demons." Prayer is what I relied on to help me through the periods of attack from the misguided natural and the evil supernatural realms.

As I compiled the information for this treatise or research study, I could comprehend why the deliverance ministry arena is still under siege today; mainly fear and a lack of understanding. Although there is an enormous amount of material published on the subject of inner healing ministry, deliverance ministry/spiritual warfare, Satan, and demonology; there is still fear, confusion, and a great deal of ignorance. In my former home church context, the subject was never approached from the pulpit, and if you dared broach anything related to evil supernaturalism, you were socially dis-fellowshipped and/or labeled as having some sort of mental disorder.

I remember what I considered my first Christian encounter with the evil supernatural. I could not understand why, that if we believed in the Father, Son (Jesus Christ) and Holy Spirit, did so many Christians seem to be so afraid of Satan and his demons. I was about twenty or twenty-one years of age at the time and wanted to confront the hordes of hell and tell them to stand down. I remember this deacon who later became an elder, that became a good friend, and mentor, would tell me to stop looking for a fight with the evil realm; I refused to listen to him.

Early one evening, I prayed to God and asked why was he allowing Satan and his demons to run wild and cause all kind of problems on the Earth, in the Church and in the lives of Christians. I demanded to be allowed to confront Satan and his demons so they could be put into their place. Let me restate, I was a young believer and fearless; some may say foolish. I was on my knees when I made that demand. At that point, I sensed, perceived, felt, detected or knew that there was an evil power in the room. I dared not get up from my knees; it was about 6:00 p.m., and I prayed until about 6:00 a.m. the next morning. That is when I no longer perceived the evil in the room.

Another major encounter was a few years after that one, when I received a call from my mother asking me to come to her home as soon as possible. When I arrived at my mother's home the front entrance door was open but the house was dark from what I could see. I proceeded to enter the house, and as I turned to the left to ascend the stairs leading to my mother's room, there was a woman at the top of the first landing whom, I did not recognize. Her hair appeared to stand straight up on her head, like Medusa, and she had a little head in her hand, and the eyes appeared to be lit up. The woman called me what I believed to be, "Beelzebub," and threw the little head at me. Before I knew it I had run out the door, leaped into my car, and was on my way. But, I heard a voice say to me, "Go back, your mother needs you." I asked God to help me and I went back into the house. The woman was still standing where she was before, still calling me names. I started up the stairs and the woman moved out of view. When I reached the first landing I could see into my mother's room. Her room had a light on, but the light seemed to be trapped in the room; it did not leak or bleed into the hallway. By the way, the little head the woman threw at me turned out to be a torn off doll's head. I cannot explain why the eyes appeared to glow.

I walked into the room; my mother was sitting up in her bed, with her back against the headboard. The woman who I still did not recognize was sitting on top of a chest of drawers, with her legs crossed and back against the mirror. She was wild and evil looking, and she began to come off of the chest of drawers. I held my hand up and told her to stop and she did. I told her I would deal with her later.

I asked my mother what was happening, she pointed to my sister who was sitting in a chair to my left drawn up in a fetal position. My two nieces who were both under three years old were on their knees speaking in what I considered gibberish. I asked my sister what was wrong and she stated that my nieces were possessed by evil spirits. I asked her who had told her that, she pointed to the woman sitting on top of the chest of drawers. I was guided by the Holy Spirit to pick my nieces up in my arms and cast out the evil spirits, which I promptly did; they stopped the gibberish. I turned and faced the woman as I was directed to do so by the Holy Spirit, and then ordered her out of my mother's house. The demon manifested for a brief moment, and then the woman left.

The last major event I want to share is when my wife, a friend, and I were on our way to church at the Masonic Temple in Detroit, Michigan. An elderly woman came up behind us as we walked and announced, "We are going to get you!" We all turned around to see what was happening. She began to shout profanities; and stated, "You in the middle, we are going to get you!" I was the one walking in the middle between my wife and my friend. I rebuked what I believed to be a demon in the name of Jesus Christ, and the women turned quietly and went on her way.

I have just shared a few of some major encounters and none of the minor ones; neither time nor space would permit what I could share; these experiences started around 1969. The point is that during a period in my Journey, I was engaged in deliverance and spiritual warfare before I was familiar with the terms; the terminology came later. I could not talk to the pastor of my home church at all, or my friends in any detail, about what I was experiencing. The Holy Spirit led me through the process.

I have known from experience that Deliverance Prayer works and has an impact on the evil supernatural. Direction from my Father in Heaven provided what I needed. The education and research has only confirmed the power of God in my life relative to inner healing and deliverance ministry, which are the major components of spiritual warfare.

My personal Deliverance Prayer journey may give some insight into my motivation. I have been prayed for by individuals with experience in deliverance ministry. I have had several experiences that range from coughing, deep breathing, falling to the floor, and the sensation that something evil was leaving my body while something good and righteous was coming in. I felt at peace and that I had been delivered from bitterness, hate, and feelings of rejection. There have been times that I felt nothing at all and did not experience reaction(s). On several occasions the experiences, sensations or reaction(s) did not manifest until later, sometimes days later. I make this statement based on the fact that the reaction(s) or behavior(s) were similar to the ones I experience while deliverance ministers were praying for me, and the behaviors I have observed while I was praying for others. I believe I needed to be delivered from the bitterness, hate and feelings of rejection I ingested in the environment of my home church, as a results of racism. I believe demonization occurred from that involvement, and that I needed and was delivered through the process of deliverance prayer and repentance, relative to bitterness, hate, and feelings of rejection. The other key component to my deliverance was forgiveness. I had to forgive everyone for real or perceived infractions/sins against me; repentance is also an element of deliverance.

My experience tells me that Deliverance Prayer is needed and necessary for everyone including Christians at all levels in the body of Christ. I have been in some debates about this whole issue of Deliverance Prayer, and one aspect I have become very interested in is the impact of a specific format of Deliverance Prayer. Could a specific format of Deliverance Prayer have impact on the person prayed for? As a pastor and a church leader, I believe that this project will be part of a process leading to a better understanding of the deliverance ministry/spiritual warfare arena, relative to impact in the form of reaction(s) and behavior(s) to a specific format of Deliverance Prayer.

Chapter Two
Theory/Literature Review

The purpose of this Theory/Literature Review chapter will be to expose the reader to a sampling of the scope of literature/information relative to the issue of deliverance and spiritual warfare, with perspectives from a cross section of authors on the subject. Another purpose would be to lay the Biblical foundation and groundwork for the research that will respond to the question of this treatise/study.

Pre-History Cosmic Conflict

I must start this discourse with some quotes from Dr. Ed Murphy, from his book *The Handbook for Spiritual Warfare*, regarding cosmic rebellion.

> Freedom of choice was given Lucifer (if that was his name), and the angels, also. In the heavenly realm all of God's angels were evidently put to the test of obedience. Although the story of that test is nowhere recorded, it is everywhere implied. Those who with stood the deception of the fallen angel, possibly Lucifer (Isa. 14:12), were confirmed in holiness. They are described as the 'holy angels' (Mark 8:38) and the 'elect angels' (I Tim. 5:21, KJV). Those who were deceived and followed the rebellious Lucifer are now, like their master, confirmed in their iniquity. According to Scripture, no provision is made for their redemption. (Murphy, 1996, p. 25)

Dr. Murphy views this account as historic fact supported by Scriptures.

This cosmic rebellion reached earth soon after man's creation. The evil it brought affected the universe on two levels: the natural and the moral. Edward J. Carnell defines *natural evil* as 'all of those frustrations of *human values* which are perpetrated, not by the free agency of man, but by the *natural elements* of the universe, such as the fury of the hurricane and the devastation of the parasite.'... Carnell defines moral evil: '[It] includes all of those frustrations of human values which are perpetrated not by the natural elements in the universe, but by the free agency of man.' In his definitions of both natural and moral evil, Carnell limits his discussion exclusively to the relationship of evil to humanity. (Murphy, 1996, p. 5 - 26)

With the introduction of humanity into the conflict between the two kingdoms, the formerly exclusive cosmic rebellion now becomes a cosmic-earthly rebellion. The historical- pictorial account is given in Genesis 3:1-24. The *historicity* of the Fall is confirmed in Scriptures such as 2 Corinthians 11:3 and Revelation 12:7-9. The historic fact of the Fall is also used by Paul in Romans 5 and I Corinthians 15 in connection with the historic, redemptive action of Jesus as the last Adam and the second man. I call Genesis 3 a pictorial account because of the vivid symbolism used to describe the historical events. The main truths of the story are just as real and historic if one admits to symbolism as they are if one follows a strict literalism. (Murphy, 1996, p. 27 - 28)

Bob Larson offers an interesting perspective regarding the cosmic conflict.

Most Christians fail to view the battle for souls as a spiritual struggle based on exacting rules of procedure, established at the dawn of creation. The devil is like a lawyer in a cosmic courtroom, arguing his case where God is the judge, eternity is at stake, and the stiffest sentence is banishment forever from the presence of God. (Larson, 1999, p. 318)

Larson presents this opinion without Biblical support, but the statement is consistent with the concept of Jesus Christ being our mediator and advocate.   Refer to I Timothy 2:5, Hebrews 12:24, Hebrews 9:14,15.

In my opinion, Boyd in his statement captures the Western mindset relative to cosmic conflict, and how one can begin to address it.

> This is the truth to which the nearly universal intuition of spiritual warfare points. Thus from the perspective of Scripture, all the so-called primitive stories of cosmic conflict, and all the supposedly primitive techniques for waging war against evil spirits, must be judged as being far more true to reality than the Western "enlightened" Worldview,   which presumptuously holds that the cosmos is strictly material, that no corporeal beings do not exist, and that humans are the highest form of life in the cosmos. If we can free ourselves from our own chronocentrism, which is in reality another form of ethnocentrism, the heavily tinted nature of our Western Enlightenment spectacles will become apparent. (Boyd, 1997, p. 19 – 20)

I think Boyd identifies the problem relative to the primary obstruction to deliverance ministry/spiritual warfare, and the understanding of the cosmic conflict in Western culture.

The warfare begins as a cosmic conflict between Lucifer and God according to Dr. Murphy and became an earthly conflict. I agree with Dr. Murphy's overview of cosmic and post cosmic-earthly spiritual warfare perspective. I submit Isaiah 14: 12 – 15, and Ezekiel 28: 11 – 19, for review.   It would be difficult to conclude that these verses refer to a human being, instead of Satan.   I think it is important to present this concept as food for thought. The option to accept, reject, or ignore can be exercised.

Spiritual Warfare
Deliverance Ministry History

Old Testament

Although this is not church history, per se, it is the earliest Biblical account of spiritual warfare according to Dr. Murphy. From my perspective, this establishes the first human encounter with what Dr. Murphy calls 'evil supernaturalism.'

> The major focus on spiritual warfare as experienced by humanity begins with Genesis 3. I will make no attempt to deal in any depth with the critical issues often raised about this story. As mentioned previously, Genesis 3 is both an historical and a pictorial account of the fall of humanity. It actually happened the way it is recorded. There really was an historical Adam and Eve. Not only were they the first human beings created in the image of God, but they stand as the representatives of the entire human race. Their transgression, particularly that of Adam as the head of the human race, is seen in Scripture as the fall of the human race (Rom.5; I Cor. 15). (Murphy, 1996, p. 34)

> Now the main teachings of the story about warfare with evil supernaturalism begins to unfold. We start with the danger of a two-way conversation, either verbally or within the mind, with the Devil on his terms. Satan began with the question, 'Has God indeed said...?' Instead of silencing him, Eve answered his question. He then subtly responded to her answer and their trap was set (Gen. 3:1 - 6). It is always dangerous to engage in a two-way dialogue with the Devil *on his terms.* To all of his doubts, lies, and boasts our response must be that of Jesus, 'Away with you, Satan! For it is written' (Matt. 4:10). 'It is written' is equivalent to 'the sword of the Spirit, which is the word (rhema) of God' of Ephesians 6:17. That is exactly how I handle demons in deliverance ministries. (Murphy, 1996, p. 35)

Spiritual warfare was not restricted to New Testament Church history; the backdrop from which this treatise has focused is New Testament spiritual warfare or deliverance. Satan was active in the Old Testament relative to opposing the human creation of God.

> And Satan stood up against Israel, and provoked David to number Israel. And David said to Joab and to the rulers of the people, Go, number Israel from Beersheba even to Dan; and bring the number of them to me, that I may know it.
>
> And Joab answered, The LORD make his people an hundred times so many more as they be: but, my lord the king, are they not all my lord's servants? why then doth my lord require this thing? why will he be a cause of trespass to Israel? (1 Chronicles 21:1-3, KJV)

I do not want to spend more time extrapolating examples from the Old Testament when my focus is New Testament spiritual warfare Deliverance Prayer. But to ignore the area totally would not have been appropriate, from a Biblical perspective. I think it sets the backdrop for an Early Church deliverance history dialogue.

New Testament

The Early Church had a solid history of deliverance relative to demonic deliverance.

> The deliverance ministry was very manifest in the early church after Pentecost. Philip, the evangelist, was credited with working miracles. 'For unclean spirits crying with a loud voice, came out of many that were possessed with them' (Acts 8:6-7). Again Paul was grieved with the spirit of divination in the young girl who kept crying out, 'These men are the servants of the Most High God which show unto us the way of salvation' (Acts 16:16-18). Today, many would applaud such utterances as great demonstrations of discernment. But Paul knew better, and after many days he commanded the spirit of divination to come out of her, and her vile employers lost their living. The evil spirit took the

best part of an hour to obey the command of Paul. But finally, they had to yield to his authority. (Whyte, 1973, p. 80)

Spiritual Warfare
Deliverance Ministry History Overview

Francis MacNutt, in my opinion, provides one of the most compelling comprehensive brief Church deliverance ministry histories in the field. I will use quotes from his book *Deliverance from Evil Spirits* extensively to complete the historical deliverance, spiritual warfare overview. My approach is to comment sparingly between quotes for transitional connectivity, and to enhance the information delivery process.

Early Church History

Early Church history reveals that many, who may have not been ordained or part of the presbytery, but were part of the general body of believers, engaged in deliverance ministry.

> In the early days of Christianity, all believers were assumed capable of praying for deliverance. Witness to this belief is the end of Mark's gospel, where the first of the five signs to 'accompany those who believe' is that 'in my name they will drive out demons' (Mark 16:17). Notice that those who perform deliverance here are not necessarily apostles or elders but ordinary believers. (MacNutt, 1995, p. 130)

Early Church fathers documented the activities of spiritual deliverance (casting out demons) through prayer, or a simple adjuration that could be invoked by any Christian. The writers included names such as Origen, Justin Martyr, Irenaeus and Tertullian:

> The ministry of exorcism continued in the early Church. After Jesus' death Philip, the deacon ordained to oversee the distribution of bread, evangelized Samaria and made a great impact: 'With shrieks, evil spirits came out many' (Acts 8:7)

After the death of the apostles, exorcisms were carried out with no mention of any special class of Christians to whom the ministry of deliverance was restricted. In fact, the Church father Origen (Martyred around A.D. 253) mentioned that many Christians cast out demons 'merely by prayer and simple adjurations which the plainest person can use. Because, for the most part, it is unlettered [or *illiterate*] persons who perform this work.' Origen added that exorcism does 'not require the power and wisdom of those who are mighty in argument.'

Justin Martyr (who wrote earlier, around A.D. 150) states that 'many Christian men' exorcise demons that cannot be cast out by pagans. Women cast out demons, too, women like St. Eugenia in the third century.

Incidentally, both Justin Martyr and Irenaeus (who wrote around A.D. 180) believed that Jews could perform exorcism in the name of the God of Abraham, Isaac and Jacob. Tertullian went so far as to say that the noblest Christian life is 'to exorcise evil spirits – to perform cures…to live to God. In his book *The Shows* he tried to convince pagans that there was more true enjoyment in casting out evil spirits and healing the sick than in attending the pagan plays and shows of the day. (Imagine a bishop encouraging his flock today to cast out evil spirits because it is more fun than seeing an R-rated movie!)

In all those early days we find no evidence that a Christian had to be ordained to cast out evil spirits. It was possible for any Christian to perform an exorcism. (MacNutt, 1995, p. 131)

Paul cast out demons Acts 16:6 –18 and Acts 19:11-12. Paul did not discuss what some might call exorcism among the gifts of the Holy Spirit. However, he did engage in spiritual deliverance warfare. Some accepted the premise that the gift of miracles included casting out demons.

> Nevertheless, Paul did not mention exorcism among the various manifestations (gifts) of the Holy Spirit enumerated in I Corinthians 12 – manifestations like 'gift of healing' (verse 9). Some believe that the gift of miracles (verse 10) might refer to exorcism. It makes sense that, just as some people are specially gifted by God with gifts of healing, other people might have gifts of exorcism. (MacNutt, 1995, p.132)

The power to cast out demons was not gender restricted in the Early Church.

> The Jesuit theologian Francisco Suarez (1548- 1617) pointed out that in the early Church, the power to cast out demons was given to all the faithful, both men and women. He also believed that the ability to exorcise the demon from a truly possessed person belonged to the order of miracles and should not be attempted 'without the special inspiration of the Holy Spirit. (MacNutt, 1995, p.132)

Note that Francisco Suarez referenced by MacNutt reinforced the concept that exorcism belonged to the order of miracles.

Narrowing of the Scope

The Church began to become narrow in the scope and practice of deliverance ministry and exorcism, limiting activity to specific groups of individuals. MacNutt suggests some reasons for the erosion of the scope relative to who should serve in the deliverance ministry activities.

> Over the course of centuries, several factors led to the gradual narrowing of exorcism to specially appointed group of exorcists. We can easily see why. For one thing, it is a difficult ministry. Even the apostles were unable to exorcise the epileptic demoniac, and they were rebuked by Jesus for being insufficiently prepared through prayer and fasting (Matthew 17:21).

> In more severe cases, insufficient spiritual protection can be dangerous to the exorcist. And if the exorcist does not know

what she is doing, it can be dangerous to the person being ministered to. Victims escaping from satanic covens are aware of this and afraid of approaching just any priest or minister for help. Their latter state could be worse than their first. (MacNutt, 1995, p. 133)

Perpetrators created a need to regulate deliverance ministry.

As a result of these dangers, Cyprian wrote in the third century about a false prophetess who acted as if she were inspired by the Holy Spirit. Then an exorcist showed up, 'a man approved,' who discerned that she was really inspired by a wicked spirit, and not the Holy Spirit. Writes Evelyn Frost:

This shows us that in the time of Cyprian there was an order of exorcists apparently regularized and approved by the Church. It is noteworthy that none of the 'very many brethren,' in spite of their strong faith, attempted to exorcise this woman, no one of the priests, but they appealed to the exorcist. This may be an indication that by the middle of the third century, the practice of exorcism in the Church had been open to abuse and required regularizing. (MacNutt, 1995, p. 133)

Problems also developed because in the Early Church history, baptism and exorcisms were connected relative to preparation for baptism (spiritual deliverance exorcism).

Another fascinating factor related to the narrowing of exorcism to a specially appointed group of exorcists is that in the early days, adult baptism (usually at Easter or Pentecost) was preceded by a long preparation period, and exorcisms were always performed as part of that preparation. (It was assumed that most, if not all, pagans required freeing from demonic influence.) Sometimes these exorcisms were performed every day during the preparation period. (MacNutt, 1995, p. 133)

More and more restrictions appeared until by the tenth century formalization began to set in.

> Notice, too, that services by the tenth century were becoming
> increasingly formalized – 'by the book,' as it were. Already
> the exorcists may have been losing out on the creative
> possibility of working individually with each demonized
> person and making up prayers tailored to that person's needs,
> instead of repeating what was in the book. (MacNutt, 1995, p.
> 134)

Restrictions continued until the Middle Ages when priests became
the ministers of deliverance and exorcisms. The process was eventually
limited to priests in the twentieth century.

> Nevertheless, the exercise of deliverance ministry became more
> and more restricted (as things usually go in the history of the
> Church), until in the Middle Ages the priest became the normal
> minister of exorcism. Finally in our own century, in the time
> of Pope Pius XI, the ministry of exorcism was limited to
> the priest. (MacNutt, 1995, p. 135)

Exorcism was deemphasized by Protestant Reformers. Laws were
passed in some cases prohibiting exorcism.

> The Protestant Reformers, for the most part, deemphasized
> exorcism or did away with it altogether. Most Calvinists
> believed that exorcism was valid only in the early days of
> Christianity. Exorcism was connected in the Reformers' mind
> with Popish superstition, and although the Anglicans
> maintained a slim belief in a need for exorcism, their 1604
> convocation passed a law 'which forbids any Anglican
> clergyman, without the express consent of his bishop obtained
> beforehand, to use exorcism in any fashion under any pretext,
> on pain of being counted an impostor and deposed from the
> ministry. (MacNutt, 1995, p. 135)

Some small pockets of deliverance ministry was practiced but
basically deliverance ministry was not encouraged. For the most part,
deliverance ministry was nonexistent or remote at best. "Still, the
deliverance ministry has, over the centuries, been gradually shut down.
In Protestant churches it has been almost abolished since, for the most part,
few believe in the necessity" (MacNutt, 1995, p.137).

One of the main reasons for the caution and restrictions on deliverance ministry - exorcism was the abuse sometimes associated with the process (i.e. the Inquisition), and the belief of some that demonic possession may just be a psychotic manifestation.

> In 1709, for instance, in a reaction against the excesses and abuses of the Inquisition, the Vatican banned five manuals of exorcism, and in 1725 it instituted extensive controls.
>
> In 1972 Pope Paul VI dropped the four minor orders, including exorcist, as steps on the way to priestly ordination, with the assumption that *exorcist* was now obsolete as an order.
>
> Part of the reason for this drop-off of belief in the need for exorcism was that experts in the field, like Fr. De Tonquedec, the official exorcist in Paris for half a century, claimed he was never convinced he had run up against a real case of possession. Instead, he said he thought that psychotics produced the symptoms of possession through their subconscious and through all the ceremonies surrounding exorcism. 'Call the devil and you'll see him; or rather not him, but a portrait made up of the sick man's ideas of him' was De Tonquedec's evaluation of his own work as official exorcist. Still in 1972 Pope Paul VI stoutly up held the traditional belief in Satan's existence. (MacNutt, 1995, p. 137)

Deliverance Resurgence
Contemporary State

The Pentecostals have been credited with the resurgence of deliverance ministry – exorcism in the twentieth century.

> Counter to the dying out of exorcism in the mainline churches, Catholic and Protestant, came the reawakening by Pentecostals of the supernatural gifts at the beginning of the twentieth century, including the power to cast out evil spirits.

The baptism of the Spirit, praying in tongues, prophecy, healing and deliverance were all awakened in a powerful way not without problems, but certainly awakened.

Emphasizing the priesthood of all believers, they did not separate the duties of clergy and laity in praying for deliverance. (MacNutt, 1995, p. 138)

The resurgence was not without problems and conflicts. Controls relative to who should perform or conduct deliverance ministry – exorcism and/or spiritual warfare reappeared. Open conflict developed between prominent individuals in the Christian arena, and Charismatic notables disputed about deliverance methodology.

But as time went on, Pentecostal churches began to exercise more authority, with only evangelists, pastors and missionaries actually performing most of the exorcisms.

The rediscovery of the need for many people to be free from demonic influence culminated in mass exorcisms – whole congregations of people under the ministry of nondenominational leaders like Derek Prince and Don Basham who taught extensively on the subject of spiritual warfare. Their mass exorcism ministry in the 1960s and '70s attracted large measure of criticism in charismatic circles, and David DuPlessis refused at times to appear on the same platform with them as a protest to their group exorcisms. Their position, though, was that exorcism had been neglected so long, and so many people needed it they had to do something, regardless of criticism, to help the many victims of demonic oppression. We were, as they saw it, in a crisis situation. (MacNutt, 1995, p.138)

Mainline churches have been impacted by the resurgence of deliverance ministry the same way they were impacted by the baptism of the Spirit doctrine.

Just as the baptism of the Spirit and a lively understanding of the ministry of laypersons spilled out into the mainline churches through the influence of pioneers like the

Episcopalian Rev. Dennis Bennett, so the gifts of healing and deliverance were introduced to mainline churches through leaders like Mrs. Agnes Sanford and the Rev. Alfred Price (one of the founders of the Order of St. Luke). (MacNutt, 1995, p.138)

Caution induced by fear has not permitted deliverance ministry to be received in the same way by mainline churches as praying in tongues, healing, and baptism in the Spirit has been received; deliverance ministry has been received with great reservation. Memories of the historical events in Salem and Medieval Europe were linked with historical and contemporary stories of failed exorcism, still breeds skepticism, control, fear, caution and disbelief.

Nevertheless, the deliverance ministry has been received by mainline denominations with more caution and criticism than the baptism in the spirit, healing and even praying in tongues. Deliverance is feared because of the disgraceful memoriess of the witch hunts of medieval Europe and the Salem witchcraft trials, coupled with recent horror stories of failed exorcism. In Germany twenty years ago, for example, two priests failed in their exorcism of a young woman, who ended up starving herself to death. The two priests and their imprudent exorcism were blamed for her death.

In any case, caution rules in all the traditional churches. In some we even see a basic disbelief in the existence of the demonic realm. (MacNutt, 1995, p 139)

It was necessary to review the deliverance ministry from what was considered Pre Church – Pre New Testament period through the Deliverance Resurgence – Contemporary state. This review provided a backdrop historically for the dynamics associated with deliverance, exorcism, spiritual warfare and supernaturalism. More time could have been dedicated for the purpose of detail, but history is not the focus of this study. Deliverance Prayer relative to impact of a specific Deliverance Prayer is the focus. My belief is thatt a historical overview supports that focus.

Biblical Foundation

I need to state here that it is not the intent of this treatise to prove that Satan/and the demons exist. That would be a separate paper, and it is not the focus of the question. To do so would detract from the focus and premise of the dialogue on deliverance prayer. I agree with M. Scott Peck, M. D.,

> The skeptical reader is likely to ask, "How can you hope to prove to me the reality of the devil when you don't even present your evidence?" The answer is that I don't hope to convince the reader of Satan's reality. Conversion to a belief in God generally requires some kind of actual encounter -- personal experience -- with the living God. Conversion to a belief in Satan is not different (Peck, 1983, p. 184).

At least one author feels that most Christians are unaware of the spirit world and the impact the physical has on the spiritual.

> Most Christians are quite unaware not only of the spirit world, but of the fact that every action we take in our physical world also affects the spirit world. Charles G. Finney describes this cause and effect relationship between the physical and spiritual world beautifully: 'Every Christian makes an impression by his conduct, and witnesses either for one side or the other. His looks, dress, whole demeanor, make a constant impression on one side or the other. He cannot help testifying for or against religion. He is either gathering with Christ, or scattering abroad.' The Last Call... For Revival, by J.T.C., p. 31. [sic] (Brown, 1992, p. 101)

I believe that Satan, demons, principalities, powers and evil spirits do exist and impact human existence, that will be the minds et from which I will proceed.

> And the seventy returned again with joy, saying, Lord, even the devils are subject unto us through thy name. And he said unto them, I beheld Satan as lightning fall from heaven. Behold, I give unto you power to tread on serpents and

scorpions, and over all the power of the enemy: and nothing shall by any means hurt you. (Luke 10:17-19, KJV)

Most of the Christians that I have encountered are unaware or in a state of disbelief. Many denominations talk about deliverance and fewer practice Deliverance Prayer from the perspective of demonic activity in the life of a believer. In fact some believe that a Christian cannot be influenced by a demon or dominated by demonic presence. This may be where the real controversy is, relative to the kinds of interpretations related to the impact connected to Deliverance Prayer, with a focus on ridding the Christian of some evil spirit's influence. This process will focus on some interpretation, but mostly on the issue of whether or not impact in the form of reaction(s) and behavior(s) would take place. Also, what would be the nature of these reaction(s), and behavior(s). With so much so called Healing and Deliverance Prayer sessions occurring in churches on television/satellite/radio, and so many styles of prayer based on denominational and nondenominational platforms; I feel it would be important to know if there is really impact that occurs to a particular format of "Deliverance Prayer." The outcome could be helpful in adding some understanding that goes beyond emotionalism, misinterpretation, manipulation and even fear on the part of some about this subject. At least within my sphere of operation some degree of clarity can be articulated based on the results. This is the purpose of my study. It would be helpful at this point to offer a definition of deliverance:

'Deliverance' means the act of expelling evil spirits or demons by adjuration in the Name of Jesus Christ through his power' (Burgess 1988, 290 [sic]). In the first act of deliverance ministry recorded in Mark, Jesus commands the unclean spirit, 'come out of him (Mark 1:25). The term 'exorcism' as a synonym of 'deliverance' is found historically in Christianity up to modern times. (Cross 1958, 485 [sic]) (Mitchell, 1999, p. 175)

This definition, in my opinion, is consistent with other authors in the arena and consistent with what Jesus Christ did in reference to spiritual deliverance.

The Spirit of the Lord is upon me, because he hath anointed me to preach the gospel to the poor; he hath sent me to heal the brokenhearted, to preach deliverance to the captives, and recovering of sight to the blind, to set at liberty them that are bruised, To preach the acceptable year of the Lord.
(Luke 4:18 – 19, KJV)

I would present that deliverance in this text implies a spiritual and literal meaning. There are some commentators that see the Luke 4:18 text as having a spiritual deliverance connotation as well as a literal one.

[1.] Deliverance to the captives, The gospel is a proclamation of liberty, like that to Israel in Egypt and in Babylon. By the merit of Christ sinners may be loosed from the bonds of guilt, and by his Spirit and grace from the bondage of corruption. It is a deliverance from the worst of thralldoms, which all those shall have the benefit of that are willing to make Christ their Head, and are willing to be ruled by him. (Henry, 1992, P.C. Bible)

[Deliverance to the captives] This is a figure originally applicable to those who were in captivity in Babylon. They were miserable. To grant deliverance to "them" and restore them to their country-- to grant deliverance to those who are in prison and restore them to their families-- to give liberty to the slave and restore him to freedom, was to confer the highest benefit and impart the richest favor. In this manner the gospel imparts favor. It does not, indeed, "literally" open the doors of prisons, but it releases the mind captive under sin; it gives comfort to the prisoner, and it will finally open all prison doors and break off all the chains of slavery, and, by preventing "crime," prevent also the sufferings that are the consequence of crime. (Barnes, 1992, P.C. Bible)

[To the captives] [aichmalootois (grk 164)]. From [aichmee], a "spear-point," and [aliskomai], "to be taken or conquered." Hence, properly, of prisoners of war.

Compare (Isa. 42:7): "To bring out captives from the prison, and those who sit in darkness from the house of restraint."

The allusion is to Israel, both as captive exiles and as prisoners of Satan in spiritual bondage. Wycliffe has: "caytifs," which formerly signified "captives." (Vincent, 1992, P.C. Bible)

I think that it is necessary to state again that these commentators point out the spiritual aspect of deliverance as well as the literal/physical aspect. However, some would like to exclude the validity of the spiritual aspect altogether. Without belaboring this point, I wanted to establish the spiritual aspect as one of the focuses of Jesus Christ relative to his ministry; which is spiritual deliverance from spiritual bondage, i.e. Satan, demons, and evil spirits.

There is a literal (freeing literal prisoner of war) meaning of deliverance and spiritual (freeing spiritual prisoner from Satan, demons, evil spirits) meaning of deliverance. I am not attempting to change the mind of anyone who may have an exclusive belief relative to the literal or spiritual meanings relative to an interpretation of the Luke 4:18 passage. But to demonstrate that some scholars articulate that the spiritual and literal interpretations have to be considered and neither is mutually exclusive. My focus is more on the spiritual interpretations or meanings.

I have utilized the book of Luke to demonstrate what Jesus did in one aspect of spiritual deliverance relative to his response to Satanic (devil and/or a demonic) influences, because of the way Luke chronicled the events. Luke recorded the occurrences in a way that seems to lead from Luke 4:18, and articulates a pattern of deliverance that did not discriminate between location, gender, and age relative to deliverance from evil spirits. Also Luke's profession as a physician, ("Luke, the beloved physician" Col. 4:14, KJV), in my opinion, gives him a scientific perspective of that day, on healing and deliverance, that may be more qualified than the other observers of that day, relative to Jesus' activities on this subject.

[Luke, the beloved physician] This was undoubtedly the author of the gospel which bears his name, and of the Acts of the Apostles. He is mentioned as the traveling companion of Paul in (Acts. 17:10), and appears to have accompanied him

afterward until his imprisonment at Rome see (2 Tim. 4:11)
(sic). (Barnes, 1992, P.C. Bible)

And came down to Capernaum, a city of Galilee, and taught
them on the Sabbath days. And they were astonished at his
doctrine: for his word was with power. And in the synagogue
there was a man, which had a spirit of an unclean devil, and
cried out with a loud voice Saying, Let us alone; what have we
to do with thee, thou Jesus of Nazareth? Art thou come to
destroy us? I know thee who thou art; the Holy One of God.
And Jesus rebuked him, saying, Hold thy peace, and come out
of him. And when the devil had thrown him in the midst, he
came out of him, and hurt him not. And they were all amazed,
and spake among themselves, saying, What a word is this! for
with authority and power he commandeth the unclean spirits,
and they come out. And the fame of him went out into every
place of the country round about. (Luke 4:31 – 37, KJV)

This area of text articulates a deliverance encounter Jesus Christ had
with a man in the synagogue, who had, "an unclean devil". The point is
that this individual was found in a well-known place of worship. In the
Twenty-first century we would call that place "church" in the Christian
context. There was a rebuke and a command from Jesus that lead to this
man's deliverance.

And it came to pass afterward, that he went throughout every
city and village, preaching and shewing the glad tidings of the
kingdom of God: and the twelve were with him, And certain
women, which had been healed of evil spirits and infirmities,
Mary called Magdalene, out of whom went seven devils…
(Luke 8:1 – 2, KJV)

This passage of scriptures, from my perspective, demonstrates that
deliverance from evil spirits is gender blind. Women are also in need of
deliverance from evil spirits. This passage also illustrates the healing
component connected to the spiritual deliverance component of the
ministry of Jesus Christ.

> And they arrived at the country of the Gadarenes, which is over against Galilee.
>
> And when he went forth to land, there met him out of the city a certain man, which had devils long time, and ware no clothes, neither abode in any house, but in the tombs. When he saw Jesus, he cried out, and fell down before him, and with a loud voice said, What have I to do with thee, Jesus, thou Son of God most high? I beseech thee, torment me not. (For he had commanded the unclean spirit to come out of the man. For oftentimes it had caught him: and he was kept bound with chains and in fetters; and he brake the bands, and was driven of the devil into the wilderness. And Jesus asked him, saying, What is thy name? And he said, Legion: because many devils were entered into him. And they besought him that he would not command them to go out into the deep. And there was there an herd of many swine feeding on the mountain: and they besought him that he would suffer them to enter into them. And he suffered them. Then went the devils out of the man, and entered into the swine: and the herd ran violently down a steep place into the lake, and were choked. (Luke 8:26 – 33, KJV)

This area of text illustrates the fact that one can be afflicted by demons outside of any situation that could be considered socially acceptable. The severity and the degree of demonic occupation articulated in this illustration, in my observation, demonstrates how destitute life can become without deliverance. Deliverance takes the form of freeing this man from multiple occupation, or "legions" of evil spirits.

> And it came to pass, that on the next day, when they were come down from the hill, much people met him. And, behold, a man of the company cried out, saying, Master, I beseech thee, look upon my son: for he is mine only child. And, lo, a spirit taketh him, and he suddenly crieth out; and it teareth him that he foameth again, and bruising him hardly departeth from him. And I besought thy disciples to cast him out; and they could not. And Jesus answering said, O faithless and perverse generation, how long shall I be with you, and suffer you?

> Bring thy son hither. And as he was yet a coming, the devil threw him down, and tare him.
>
> And Jesus rebuked the unclean spirit, and healed the child, and delivered him again to his father. (Luke 9:37 – 42, KJV)

This passage of scripture demonstrates that youth is not an immunization from demonic attack. This passage of scripture also indicates that the rebuking of an unclean spirit can also be construed as a healing.

> And the seventy returned again with joy, saying, Lord, even the devils are subject unto us through thy name. And he said unto them, I beheld Satan as lightning fall from heaven. Behold, I give unto you power to tread on serpents and scorpions, and over all the power of the enemy: and nothing shall by any means hurt you.
>
> Notwithstanding in this rejoice not, that the spirits are subject unto you; but rather rejoice, because your names are written in heaven. (Luke 10: 17 – 20, KJV)

The passage of scripture reveals the fact that Jesus Christ authorized power over the enemy, which is Satan; one of the names used to describe Satan is serpent. (Revelation 12:9, New King James, NKJ)

The Scriptures are clear on what Christ did and the reaction(s) he got. The disciples also realized some kind of reaction(s), Luke 10:17 - 20. The Biblical example in Luke is subject to interpretation, but they are there and clearly show activity relative to evil spirits.

There were other scriptures that discuss what Jesus and the disciples did relative to intervention, activity, dialogue and deliverance concerning the demonic realm: Matthew 4:24, Matthew 17:18, Mark 1: 23 – 26, Mark 3: 11 – 12, Mark 3:22, Mark 5:12 – 13, Mark 6: 13, Mark 16: 17, Luke 4: 40 – 41, Luke 6: 17 – 18, John 8:44, I Peter 5:8, James 3:14 – 15. The apostle Paul made it clear that this was not a war of flesh and blood, but a war of spirit. " For we wrestle not against flesh and blood, but against principalities, against powers, against the rulers of the darkness of this world, against spiritual wickedness in high places " (Ephesians 6:12, KJV). "For though we walk in the flesh, we do not war after the flesh..." (2 Corinthians 10:3, KJV).

There is a Biblical foundation for spiritual warfare and deliverance relative to demonic activity.

Some Deliverance Arena Controversies and Arguments

The subject of deliverance is one surrounded by controversies that still exists today, fueled by ignorance and fear. Churches are slow to embrace the concept of spiritual deliverance, Satan and/or evil spirits.

Fear of Satan, Demons and Evil Spirits

Ing is one of several authors that articulates the fear factor of evil spirits and ignorance relative to deliverance from demons, as a problem in the acceptance of deliverance ministry or casting out demons.

> Many churches shy away from the subject of deliverance or casting out demons. Some claim that by talking about the devil, we give him glory. Others are simply afraid of the subject. Still others don't believe in evil spirits or in a personal Satan. Most speak largely out of ignorance and fear. (Ing, 1996, p. 7)

Ing expresses an opinion that I concur with based on experience with churches and Christians regarding Satan, demons and /or evil spirits.

Whyte discusses deliverance from demon and evil spirits as a neglected ministry by the Christian church. He also points out that deliverance ministry is becoming more prominent.

> The ministry of casting our demons, or evil spirits, is one, which has long been neglected by the Christian church, probably owing to fear of the unknown. It is, however, a ministry which is coming more and more into prominence in this latter day revival. (Whyte, 1973, p. 63 - 64)

Whyte identifies fear as the probable cause as to why the Christian church ignores this ministry. I agree with what Whyte states about the latter day revival prominence of deliverance ministry.

Mitchell points out that fear is irrational relative to the Devil. The demons should have fear, because of the power of God in us through Jesus Christ.

> Therefore Jesus is saying, 'No defense [sic] that Satan puts up can stand against my church.' Yet the tragic facts of church history show that all too often Christians have been terrified of the defensive gates of Hades! Deere's words express the truth clearly: 'All fear of the devil is irrational fear. No Christian should ever fear Satan or any demon. The only person a Christian is taught to fear in the New Testament is God himself.' Believers should recognize that behind the devil's vulnerable defenses [sic] demons shudder! (James 2:19) (Mitchell, 1999, p. 11)

I am with Mitchell relative to believers recognizing how vulnerable the demonic defenses are to the power of God.

Ing, Whyte and Mitchell discuss the resistance of the Christian arena to address or fully embrace the ministry of spiritual deliverance, relative to Satan and evil spirits.

They attribute the resistance to fear of the unknown, lack of belief in evil spirits, and the belief that deliverance ministry gives the devil glory. I have encountered these attitudes and would agree with the authors.

There is another mindset relative to fear of demons and evil spirits that would fall into a category described by Sigmund Freud.

> Wundt remarks that 'among the influences which myth everywhere ascribes to demons the evil ones preponderate, so that according to the religions of races evil demons are evidently older than good demons.' Now it is quite possible that the whole conception of demons was derived from the

extremely important relation to the dead. In the further course of human development the ambivalence inherent in this relation then manifested itself by allowing two altogether contrary psychic formations to issue from the same root, namely, the fear of demons and of ghosts, and the reverence for ancestors. (Freud, 1966, p.857 – 858)

This is a different perspective relative to the aspect of fear relative to demons and the demon concept. This perspective comes from the mind of a psychoanalyst. His argument points to contrary psychic formations proceeding from the same roots that discusses fear of demons, ghosts, and ancestral reverence, is interesting. I adhere to the pro deliverance, fear of demons, perspectives of Ing, Whyte and Mitchell.

Possession and Demonization

There also seems to be an issue of whether or not a Christian can be possessed or demonized. Part of the problem according to Richard Ing is translation.

Others claim that when we become Christians, we are cleansed of all demons. The Bible does not say that. It says that our sins are washed away by the blood, but does not mention demons.

It is true, however, that demons cannot 'possess' us. Unfortunately, the King James Version of the Bible uses an incorrect word. The correct word is 'demonization,' or having demons. Possession implies total control. Demons cannot possess us, but we can possess demons.

A quick fix for the issue is the contention that demons can only cling on from the outside. However, the Bible does not say that Jesus and the disciples 'brushed off,' 'rubbed off,' or 'chased off' demons. Instead, the Bible consistently says,

'cast out.' 'Cast out' clearly indicates that demons were 'in.'
To get something out, it has to first be in. (Ing, 1996, p. 13)

H.A. Maxwell Whyte was also concerned with the use of the term
"possessed;" and the whole question relative to someone being
possessed.

> The very phrasing of this question is unfortunate. The
> question is usually asked in a derogatory manner by those
> who totally reject the idea that a born-again Christian could
> ever be troubled or afflicted by a demon.
>
> The problem revolves around the use of the word *possessed*, a
> word that suggests the demon totally inhabits and owns the
> sufferer with no area free and with free will absolutely
> blocked.
>
> I do not believe a born-again Christian can be possessed by a
> demon. The very idea of a Christian who loves the Lord
> being *owned and controlled* by a demon is totally abhorrent
> and unacceptable. If Christians would abandon the use of this
> confusing word "possessed" and speak of demon problem in
> terms of 'oppressions,' 'vexations,' or 'bindings,' believers
> would avoid a lot of confusion. (Whyte, 1989, p. 101)

Some authors and clergy, who believed that a Christian could not be
demonized, but had experiences in the field and in their personal lives
that mandated a review of their non-demonization of Christians position.

> As evangelicals, we are committed to accepting whatever the
> Bible asserts. But understanding precisely what it says is
> often difficult. For example, for years Murphy and I believed
> that the following biblical verse and several others proved that
> Christians could not be demonized: 'But you belong to God, my
> children, and have defeated the false prophets, because the
> Spirit who is in you is more powerful that the spirit in those who
> belong to the world' (I John 4:4).
>
> I believe this Scripture. And I wish with all my heart that my
> earlier interpretation of it were right, that Christians can not

be demonized.   But experience has shown me that the verse cannot mean that the presence of the Holy Spirit within Christians makes it impossible for dark angels to live in them. The process by which I free persons from demons proves the truth of this verse over and over, but I have had to reconsider my interpretation of it. (Kraft, 1992, pg. 61)

Kraft believes there are two reasons confusion and conflict exist relative to demons and Christians being influenced, infested, possessed, or demonized.   Kraft also believes Christians can have indwelling demons.

> The discussion over whether Christians can have demons living within them stems from two sources: the terms that are used and the lack of experience within the Christian community in delivering people from demons.

> …The concept of 'demon possession' has gained credibility through a poor translation of Greek terms referring to people who have demons living within them. If 'possession' is used at all, it should label only those who are so totally controlled by demons that their whole being is taken over by the alien personality from time to time. I have never met, and only rarely heard of a 'Christian for whom 'possessed' could even be considered appropriate.

> The deliverance ministries of my acquaintance, however, agree that Christians can have demons living within them. (Kraft, 1992, p. 63 - 64)

Prince agrees with Kraft that Christians can be in a condition that requires deliverance from demons. His position is that he has never been exposed to a Scriptural presentation that proves Christians cannot be demonized.

> In more than thirty years, I have never heard or read a reasoned, scriptural presentation of the doctrinal position that Christians can never need deliverance from demons. Those who believe this, as I said this in Chapter 5, seem to consider it so obvious that it needs no support from Scripture. But the

implications of such a position can be, to say the least, surprising. (Prince, 1998, p. 142)

However, there are some that do not agree with the premise that Christians can have indwelling demons or be possessed. The attitude is that demons can attack from without but not from within.

> Jesus didn't teach his disciples or anyone else for that matter, how to cast out demons out of true believers. In fact, there is no account in the Bible of a true believer being demon possessed. Isn't that strange in the light of the all the demons supposedly being cast out of Christian believers today?
>
> This is not to say that Christians can't be attacked from without by demons in the mind, will, emotions and body. They can be troubled, pressed, buffeted, harassed, depressed, obsessed, oppressed, in bondage and bruised and **still not be possessed by the devil.** (Robeson & Robeson, 1997, p. 63)

One speculative argument proposes that Christians would be the most likely target for demonic attack because they pose the greater threat to Satan. Therefore demonization of Christians is a logical warfare strategy for Satan and the demons to pursue.

> If you were Satan, on whom would you spend your time? What kind of priority would Satan likely give to disrupting the lives and ministries of church people: High priority, I should think. For these are the ones who could hurt the satanic kingdom if they got free. (Kraft, 1992, p. 29)

There may be a distinction between exorcism and deliverance. MacNutt believes there is a distinction, and that distinction makes exorcism rare and deliverance common.

> "Something as severe and dangerous as exorcism requires not us but experts. The problem is, while the need for exorcism is rare, the need for deliverance is common" (MacNutt, 1995, p. 67).

At least one author feels that theological arguments must yield to experience. I would agree with Ing's position relative to experience and theological arguments.

> Theological arguments must give way to experience. Even scientists are known to abandon pet theories when actual experiences do not support them. Over 99% of the people I have delivered have been born-again tongue -speaking Christians, including many charismatic pastors. If you do not believe that Christians can have demons, I suggest you attend a number of deliverance sessions. Don't pass judgment until you have investigated the matter thoroughly. It is important to know the truth in these end times. If demons can reside in the human body, then they need to be cast out. (Ing, 1996, p. 13)

I would agree with the argument that a Christian can be possessed by demons and fall under partial or complete control of the demon(s). I also agree that Satan can enter and control a human being. Note in John 13:26 - 27 it states,

> Jesus answered, He it is, to whom I shall give a sop, when I have dipped it. And when he had dipped the sop, he gave it to Judas Iscariot, the son of Simon. And after the sop Satan entered into him. Then said Jesus unto him, That thou doest, do quickly. (John 13:26 – 27, KJV)

Worley believes that in the name of Jesus we have authority over every demon spirit. Worley also feels that if a person has an area in their life that is un-surrendered to Christ the demons can maintain control over that part of the person's life.

> Although believers wielding the name of Jesus have authority over every demon spirit, they cannot coerce the human will. In dealing with individuals Jesus did not violate the human will. We have had cases where deliverance was proceeding smoothly until some spirit (discerned by the workers) was rebuked and commanded to manifest and to leave. When this concerned an area un-surrendered to the Lord, the person

immediately emerged and the demon was released from pressure. Deliverance ceased immediately, and most of the time the person became angry and upset. (Worley, 1976, p. 126)

Worley implies that control, relative to demonic spirits, is based on surrendered and un-surrendered areas of that person's life to the Lord. His assertion is that Jesus did not violate the human will relative to deliverance, and freedom from demonic spirits.

It would appear that Worley is saying that the level, degree or totality of demonic spiritual control is predicated on the degree that a person has surrendered their life or areas of their life to Jesus Christ. The question of demonic or satanic levels of control may not be an argument of demonization or possession, but an argument of surrendered areas of one's life that may dictate levels of control, from external irritation to full scale internal possession.

My position remains the same as stated before I referenced Worley. In my opinion, Worley is basically stating that the level or degree of demonization and possession is a human will - submission to God issue. I think his argument has some merit.

Principalities and Powers

"For we wrestle not against flesh and blood, but against principalities, against powers, against the rulers of the darkness of this world, against spiritual wickedness in high places" (Ephesians 6:12, KJV). The principalities and powers text is often discussed in context with the putting on the armor of God in Ephesians 6:13. Frangipone asserts that the heavenly places is a battleground arena where we should be prepared to do battle.

> "Thus, our purpose here is to help equip you for battle in each of the three primary battlegrounds: the mind, the church and the heavenly places" (Frangipane, 1989, p. 7).

Eckhardt reinforces the same mind set as part of the apostolic anointing. He also contends that the principalities and powers must be challenged.

> The first thing the Lord gave the Twelve when He sent them out was 'power against unclean spirits' (Matt. 10: 1 (KJV). The apostolic anointing is therefore recognized in the spirit realm. A level of power – an authority that is released through apostles and apostolic churches –must be acknowledged by the demonic and angelic realm. ...The principalities and powers that have gripped multitudes of people for so long must be challenged by implementing this kind of power and authority. (Eckhardt, 1998, p. 50)

Frangiopane and Eckhardt imply more than just a deliverance ministry for individuals who may be demonically afflicted, but as warriors battling the entire spirit realm; whenever they attempt to influence, manipulate, and control whenever they choose to manifest.

> Weber supports the spirit warrior premise.

> Everywhere the New Testament insists the Christian life is about being a faithful warrior. The Christian life is about fighting the good fight, waging war, and wrestling or struggling with a fierce, implacable enemy. The fight of the Christian man or woman is the life of a spirit warrior. (Weber, 2001, p. 11)

The spirit warrior has to be concerned with principalities and powers that have vast influence. Garrison articulates the span of influence that sometimes operates unseen, without bodies.

> Notice that we are the ones expected to wrestle. We are not fighting people made of flesh and blood, but against unseen persons without bodies...great evil princes...huge numbers of evil spirits. We are fighting principalities...rulers, leaders, executives, chiefs, heads, masterminds, controllers, and main strongmen. (Garrison, (1980, p, 38)

Wink comments on the powers from the perspective of manifestations.

Every Power tends to have a visible pole, and outer form – be it a church, a nation, or an economy – and an invisible pole, an inner spirit or driving force that animates, legitimates, and regulates its physical manifestation in the world. (Wink, 1984, p. 5)

Wink implies that the powers operate through churches, nations, and economies from the invisible realm.

McAlpine submits what he identifies as four traditions that attempt to understand the scriptural context of principalities and powers relative to mission in the Christian life.

Christians concerned for mission and living in the midst of these upheavals are returning to what Scripture has to say about the principalities and powers. They are doing so within various traditions. ...The Reformed, Anabaptist, third wave, and social science traditions have struggled to understand the role of the principalities and powers in mission. (McAlpine, 1991, p. 75)

A more complete description of the traditions can be reviewed in Appendix A under McAlpine. I would lean toward the Anabaptist tradition.

In my opinion, Wylie-Kellerman makes an important statement regarding the principalities and powers in their manifested forms, and the failure of moral theology in the American context to confront them.

What is most crucial about this situation, biblically speaking, is the failure of moral theology, in the American context, to confront the principalities – the institutions, systems, ideologies, and other political and social powers – as militant, aggressive, and immensely influential creatures in this world as it is. (Wylie-Kellerman, 1991, p. 71)

Relative to principalities and powers I argue with the authors and believe that this is a major battleground in the deliverance ministry/spiritual warfare arena. I believe prayer is the major weapon in engaging the principalities and powers in all their invisible and physical manifestations. As far as Christians are concerned Church is one "outer form," (Wink, 1984) where the principalities and powers can be confronted and ultimately defeated.

Demons and Mental Illness

Before I move on to another section of this treatise, I need to briefly address the issues of mental/psychological illness and demonization. This is an issue of great controversy; Kraft views this controversy from two perspectives which he calls myths 4 and 5.

> Myth 4: DEMONIZATION IS SIMPLY PSYCHOLOGICAL ILLNESS
>
> Liberal Christians assume that the biblical accounts of Jesus casting out demons simply record Jesus' way of dealing with psychological illness. "Jesus simply accommodated to the belief of the people of that day that demons caused problems," they say. "He knew then what we know now that the so-called demonized were really heavy-duty psychological cases."
>
> Unfortunately, variations of this myth are common among evangelicals as well. Our naturalistic Western worldview (see Kraft, *Christianity with Power*) makes it extremely difficult for us to believe supernatural beings such as Satan and demons are real. We are taught as we grow up that 'seeing is believing" and "if you can't see it, it doesn't exist." Invisible beings with power are all right in fairy tales, but they have no place in real life. (Kraft, 1992, p. 39 – 40)

Kraft also addresses what he considers the other extreme of the demons being the cause of every emotional problem. In fact, Kraft believes that demons rarely cause emotional problems.

MYTH 5: ALL EMOTIONAL PROBLEMS ARE CAUSED
BY DEMONS

In reaction to myth four, many who discover that demons really
exists often go the opposite extreme. They begin to believe
that all emotional problems (and most others as well) are caused
by demons. This is the "lunatic fringe" position of many
Pentecostals and Charismatics. And it turns off large numbers
of both Christians and non-Christians to even considering the
possibility that demons exist and are active.

Though I contend that demonization is very common, it is
clear to me that emotional problems are seldom if ever caused
by demons. The origins of such difficulties lies elsewhere.
When a child is abused, for example, though a demon may be
pushing the abuser, *it is the abuse, not the demon, that causes
problems in the child.* (Kraft, 1992, p. 40 - 41)

Wink makes a statement regarding Satan, demons and mental illness.

Satan is not an independent agent. He has his own satanic
host. He is 'the prince of demons.' Demons, however, are
the drunk uncle of the twentieth century: we keep them out of
sight. Modern psychiatry had explained them all away as
primitive approximations of mental illnesses now more
exactly named, if not, arguably, better treated, by modern
drugs and therapies. (Wink, 1986, p. 41)

Wink also comments on what he calls three types of demonic
manifestations.

I will propose that there are three types of demonic
manifestations: outer personal possession, collective
possession, and the inner personal demonic. By outer
personal possession I mean the possession of an individual by
something that is alien and extrinsic to the self. By collective
possession I mean the possession of groups or even nations by
a god or demon capable of bending them as one in the service
of death. And by the inner personal demonic I mean the

struggle to integrate a split-off or repressed aspect that is intrinsic to the personality, an aspect that is only made evil by its rejection. (Wink, 1986, p. 43)

Wink explains inner personal demons in a way that resembles a mental health or mental illness diagnosis.

By the inner personal demonic I mean a split-off or unintegrated aspect of the self which is not alien, but intrinsic to the personality, and which needs to be owned, embraced, loved, and transformed as part of the struggle for wholeness. This is not equivalent to the New Testament accounts of possession. Those seem to have been alien influences not integral to the self—elements introjected into the personality from the general pathology of society—what I am calling outer personal demons. (Wink, 1986, p. 52)

Another author, Dr. M. Scott Peck, addresses this same issue under the heading, "Mental Illness and the Naming of Evil." This author address evil and psychological disorders from a classification or category perspective. Should evil be considered a psychiatric disorder? That is one of the major questions raised.

If evil is to be named a psychiatric disorder, is it sufficiently unique to stand in a category all by itself or does it fit into one of the already existing categories? Surprisingly, in view of the degree to which it has been neglected, the present system of classification of psychiatric illness seems quite adequate for the simple addition of evil as a sub-category. The existing broad category of personality disorders currently covers those psychiatric conditions in which the denial of personal responsibility is the predominate feature. By virtue of their unwillingness to tolerate the sense of personal sin and the denial of their imperfection, the evil easily fit into this broad diagnostic category. (Peck, 1983, p.128)

It should be understood that when Peck discusses evil it is not totally detached from the concept of the devil, and goodness is not detached totally from the concept of God.

Bear in mind also that just as the issue of evil inevitably raises the question of the devil, so the inextricable issue of goodness raises the question of God and creation. While we can – and, I believe, should – bite off little pieces of mystery upon which to gnash our scientific teeth, we are approaching matters vast and magnificent beyond our comprehension. (Peck, 1983, p. 42)

Evil, then, for the moment, is that force, residing either inside or outside of human beings, that seeks to kill life or liveliness. And goodness is its opposite. Goodness is that which promotes life and liveliness. (Peck, 1983, p. 43)

I think this dialogue demonstrates a struggle relative to evil, and good in the context of mental disorder as it relates to devil induced evil, and God induced goodness. Dr. Ed Murphy addresses the common church attitude regarding mental illness.

The name mental illness is unfortunate. It gives the impression that one is crazy, emotionally weak, too cowardly to cope with life. No truly born again believer can become mentally ill, we are often told. He has the mind of Christ so how could his mind become ill? A believer who becomes mentally ill has sin in his life. It is the believer's own fault. If he would only break with the sin patterns in his life, stop worrying and trust God, he would become well.

The victims of mental illness too often don't find much comfort, sympathy, or help from Christians or churches. Every organ in the believer's body can become diseased or break down but not his brain or mind. Somehow that cannot happen to a genuine believer. (Murphy, 1996, p. 485)

This debate demonstrates the volatile attitudes that exist toward this subject. The caution is not to slip into a mode where people are labeled one way or another, to the point of being excluded from the deliverance or treatment they may need.

White [Dr. John White, Christian psychiatrist] observes that doctors often refer depressed Christians to him, but pastoral counselors seldom do so...White continues with the problem Christians have with accepting the fact that believers can suffer depressive illnesses. ... We dare not slip into the "all things are spiritual' mode. Some mood disorders and mental brain-psychological malfunctions among believers are not due to spiritual problems but to natural factors. (Murphy, 1996, p. 488)

I think it is important not to exclude the possibility of demon activity or naturally induced mental disorders when attempting to diagnose the source of behavioral dysfunction.

Wink articulates the belief that Jesus was not relating to stories of exorcism relative to inner personal demons, but instruction relative to inner evil.

The biblical reference point for inner personal demons is not the stories of exorcisms, but Jesus' instruction concerning inner evil:

Hear me, all of you, and understand: there is nothing outside a person which by going in can defile; but the things which come out are what defile. ...

For from within, out of the human heart, come evil thoughts, fornication, theft, murder, adultery, coveting, wickedness, deceit, licentiousness, envy, slander, pride, foolishness. All these evil things come from within, and these are what defile. (Mark 7:14 – 15, 21 – 23, ILL)

Jesus does not subscribe to the opinion that our emotions or habits can or should be cast out by exorcism. To attempt to cast out something essential to the self is like performing castration to deal with lust. Great harm is done by well-intended, self –appointed 'exorcists,' largely in neo - Pentecostal circles, by exorcising people who are not genuinely possessed (that is, are not possessed by outer personal or collective demons). (Wink, 1986, p. 52)

I agree with Wink in part, relative to the statement that every evil aspect of our personality is not demon induced, but could be a matter of fleshly emotions and habits of the individual.

I agree with Dr. Murphy relative the need of more insight yielding research.

> Finally, I am convinced that everyone, the author included, is in need of further insight into the relationship between the spirit world and mental illness. Much has been written about the spirit world, even more about mental illness. We need a book, which treats both subjects and show how each is related to the other. If God wills, I may attempt to write such a book. (Murphy, 1996, p. 490)

My position is that the references in Luke are clear about the demonic evil activity that Jesus encountered. Nowhere in that group of Scripture is there any implication that the problems were naturally induced mental disorders; I must proceed from that perspective. This is not to imply that the abilities and/or skills were present or absent to distinguish between demonic activity or mental disorder. I must accept that Jesus Christ had the ability to know the difference.

The focus of this study is to document the impact in the form of reaction(s) and behavior(s) to a specific format of Deliverance Prayer. The aspect of mental illness versus demonic influence was addressed because it is a debate in the spiritual warfare arena but not a debate to be resolved by this study. The reader has the right and the obligation to draw their own conclusion on the issue, I have.

World View

World view in the context of religion focuses on the spiritual and the material; some may state it as the supernatural and natural. The world has a perception relative to an overall belief about what controls or influence existence, what is considered real or realistic or what is not. I have selected several authors' perspectives, Dr. L. David Mitchell's, Dr. Ed Murphy's and Walter Wink's relative to World view.

Dr. L. David Mitchell

By 'world view' we mean that mental framework which gives shape to our existence. Our world view integrates our knowledge and understanding of this world, our perceptions about human life, about moral social realities, and about our reason for existence. For Christians, as for humankind naturally, the realm of spiritually good and evil is part of their world view. (Mitchell, 1999, p. 31)

God and the realm of angels, with Satan and his demons, provide the spiritual background, the framework against which men and women and children live out their lives. Their lives are, in turn, not only physical lives in a material world, but spiritual ones. In every human heart there is a 'nostalgia' for heaven and a reality that is far greater than all we presently see. Every human being has a sense of the numinous, of the transcendent and righteous Creator.

For the practitioner of 'primal religion', the animist, every occurrence is fraught with spiritual meaning. The universe is open with a blurred line between natural and supernatural. The material world integrates with the realm of gods and spirits. (Mitchell, 1999, p. 30)

Mitchell discusses physical lives in a material world being spiritual lives as well. He proposes that the universe is open, having a blurred line between natural and supernatural, integrating with dimension of gods, and spirits. I could accept this world view concept.

Dr. Ed Murphy

Aside from the agnostic position, only two conceivable world views exist.

The *spiritualistic world view* affirms that ultimate reality is spiritual: immaterial, not physical or material. According to this view; whether ultimate reality is looked upon as personal or impersonal, it is spiritual. The vast majority of the world's more than five billion inhabitants hold to some form of a spiritualistic world view. Intellectually convinced atheists are very rare even in Western and in Marxist societies. Ours is not a world of philosophical materialists, but of convinced spiritualists. (Murphy, 1996, p. 3)

Second, the materialistic or naturalistic world view affirms that ultimate reality is material or physical, not spiritual. This view assumes that all life generated spontaneously from non-life and that by this process primitive single-celled life forms evolved over vast periods of time in to the vast range of life as we know it today. (Murphy, 1996, p. 4)

Murphy setting aside the agnostic perspective dialogues on the spiritual and materialistic world views. He asserts that the vast majority of the World's population, about five billion hold to some kind of variation of the spiritual world view concept as he has outlined it to be. I could subscribe to the spiritualistic world view as articulated by Murphy.

Walter Wink

Wink identifies five World view perspectives:

The Ancient Worldview [sic]. This is the worldview reflected in the Bible... In this conception everything earthly has its heavenly counterpart, and everything heavenly has its earthly counterpart. Every event is thus a simultaneity of both dimensions of reality. (Wink, 1992, p. 4)

This world view concept is in my opinion is simplistic and consistent with my theology.

The Spiritualistic Worldview. What distinguishes this worldview...from all other types is that it divides human beings into 'soul' and 'body'; one understands oneself as the same as one's 'soul' and other than one's 'body.'In this account, the created order is evil, false, corrupted. Creation was itself the fall. Matter is either indifferent or downright evil Earthly life is presided over by imperfect and evil Powers. (Wink, 1992, p. 4)

I have some problems with this concept relative to creation being the fall. Also, the statement relative to the evil and corrupted nature of the created order, presents a problem relative to the theological paradigm I subscribe to.

> *The Materialistic Worldview.* This view... became prominent in the Enlightenment, but is as old as Democritus (ca. 460-ca. 370 B.C.E.), and is in Many ways the antithesis of the world-rejection of spiritualism. In this view, there is no heaven, no spiritual world, no God, no soul—nothing but material existence and what can be known through the five senses and reason. The spiritual world is an illusion. (Wink, 1992, p. 5)

This world view perspective is the opposite of everything I would adhere to as a Christian and theologian – no heaven, no spiritual world, no soul, or God; only an existence of the five senses and reason.

> *The 'Theological' Worldview.* In reaction to materialism, Christian theologians invented the supernatural... Acknowledging that this supersensible realm could not be known by the senses, they conceded earthly reality to modern science and preserved a privileged 'spiritual' realm immune to confirmation or refutation—at the cost of an integral view of reality and the simultaneity of heavenly and earthly aspects of existence. (Wink, 1992, p. 5)

This world view concept is not consistent with the theological concepts I embrace. The idea that Christian invented supernaturalism, this precludes the ideology that God is the supernatural being who created the natural as well as the supernatural realm.

> An Integral Worldview. This new worldview... is emerging from a confluence of sources: the reflections of Carl Jung, Telhard de Chardin, Morton Kelsey, Thomas Berry, Matthew Fox, process philosophy, and the new physics. It sees everything as having an outer and an inner aspect. It attempts

to take seriously the spiritual insights of the ancient or biblical worldview by affirming a withinness or interiority in all things, but sees this inner spiritual reality as inextricably related to an outer concretion or physical manifestation. It is no more intrinsically 'Christian' than the ancient worldview, but I believe it makes the bible data more intelligible for people today than any other available worldview, including the ancient (Wink, 1992, p. 5)

This world view is also one that reflects dimensions of my theology and Christianity. I could embrace this world view cautiously.

From my perspective, time spent with the world view concept relative to Christianity is important to this treatise on Deliverance Prayer. The issue of spiritual warfare exorcism, demonization is impacted by the world view that focuses on spiritual and the material, or the natural and the supernatural. It is important to understand what the thinking is from a global perspective. I subscribe to the Spiritualistic World View, proposed by Murphy. Note how the Spiritualistic World View proposed by Murphy differs from the one proposed by Wink. I would also state that Mitchell describes a mindset that I could embrace without conflict. The Ancient World View and the Integral World View would also fit into my philosophy. These four world view positions that I have selected to embrace best describe how I operate relative to inner healing and deliverance ministry/spiritual warfare.

Traditional African Religious Rituals and Practices

Introduction

It is important that some dialogue is devoted to traditional African deliverance-like rituals and customs. Africans who came into the United States as slaves, brought with them religious rituals of their African heritage. This is significant because a review reveals some of the traditional African religious rituals and practices have surfaced in religious arenas in America. From my perspective dialogue relative to African deliverance-like religious ritual activity will be useful in understanding the deliverance ministry/spiritual warfare arena, and the possible impact that the African culture may have had on the basic deliverance ministry/spiritual warfare model we see today.

It is also important to note that the Pentecostal/Charismatic movement gained World attention and recognition through William J. Seymour, the son of former slaves.

"William J. Seymour was born in Centerville Louisiana on May 2, 1870. He was the son of former slaves, Simon and Phyllis Seymour. Even after gaining their freedom the Seymour's had continued working on the plantation" (Joyner, n.d., p. 3).

The Pentecostal/Charismatic Movement began under the leadership of a black man, and with a small group of black people. They freely shared what they had been given, and were delighted when they saw the Spirit poured out on those from other races, especially whites. They felt that the Lord had given them the greatest gift, and they were thrilled that they were able to share it with their white brethren. That this great worldwide revival was a contribution from the black community has never been denied by white Pentecostals, but is often forgotten.(Joyner, n.d., p. 7).

The Azuza Street Revival of 1906, was founded by William J. Seymour, and as a point of documented history influenced the Founder of the Church of God in Christ, Charles Harrison Mason and the Founder of the Assemblies of God, Eurdorus N. Bell. The importance of the continuous impact of William J. Seymour and what occurred as a result of the Azuza Street Revival has significantly influenced the entire church.

It is impossible to understand the present state of Christianity without understanding both the past and continuing impact of the Pentecostal Movement. To even call what began at Azusa Street just a revival would be to obscure its true importance. It was a revival, but it was also a renewal and a reformation of the church as well. With the possible exception of Luther's Reformation, there probably has not been another movement in church history which has had a greater overall impact on the entire church.

This impact is not only continuing, it is continuing to increase. Through the Pentecostal Revival and the subsequent Neo-Pentecostal movements spawned from it such as the Charismatic Renewal, already more ministers of the gospel have been ordained, more missionaries have been sent out, more churches have been planted, and more people have been brought to salvation than through any other movement in church history. (Joyner, n.d., p. 1).

The growth factor is another indication of the level of influence that is still being realized as a result of the Azuza Street Revival. "Taken as a group, the Pentecostal/Charismatic Movements are now the second largest category in all of Christianity. If their present rate of growth is sustained, they will, in just a few years, outnumber the rest of Christianity combined" (Joyner, n.d., p. 1).

The Pentecostal/Charismatic movement bares some similarities to African religious rituals: such as "glossolalia" or speaking in tongues, baptism of the spirit, the ecstatic praise, worship, and dance.

Geographical Focus

Slaves were seized from Central, South, East, and West Africa. For the purpose of identification relative to this review, it is necessary to pinpoint the location from which most slaves in America came. According to Albert J. Raboteau, that region is West Africa and Congo-Angola region.

Over the four centuries of the Atlantic trade, slaves were seized from many parts of Africa –Central, South and East— as well as West Africa. The problem of the provenience of American slaves is a difficult one, complicated by the lengthy duration of the trade. ...slaves bound for the Americas came from many different nations, tribes, and language groups. ...it is clear that a large percentage of American slaves came from West Africa and from the Congo-Angola region.

> This vast territory stretched along the coast from Senegambia in the northwest to Angola in the southeast; it extended several hundred miles inland, and embraced societies and cultures as diverse as those of the Mandinke, the Yoruba, the Ibo and Bakongo. (Raboteau, 1978, p.7)

Among the traditional religions of the West African people, there were and still exist too many significant religious variations that would prohibit single categorization.   However, similar basic principles, commonality of religious patterns, and spiritual modes of perception could be identified in different West African religions.

> There were, and are, too many significant differences among the religions of various West African peoples, not to mention local variations within any single people, to permit putting them all into a single category.   However, similar modes of perception, shared basic principles, and common patterns of ritual were widespread among different West African religions. (Raboteau, 1978, p.7)

In the midst of vast diversity, there was enough similarity to compose a general composite of traditional West African religious rituals and practices.

> Beneath the diversity, enough fundamental similarity did exist to allow a general description of the religious heritage of African slaves, with supplemental information concerning particular peoples, such as the Akan, Ewe, Yoruba, Ibo and others, whose influence upon the religions of Afro-Americans have long been noted. (Raboteau, 1978, p.7 - 8)

Traditional religious ritual deliverance-like activity from the West African region will be the focus. According to Raboteau, this region will provide some accurate elements of impact on the United States of America, relative to some religious practices. I think it is important to point out that the contemporary deliverance ministry/spiritual warfare reawakening is a product of the Pentecostal/Charismatic movement. (MacNutt, 1999) Although the focus is not on religious rituals of slaves in America, it is important to narrow the field of discussion to a region where slaves did originate relative to the United States. This approach would be more germane to the overall treatise/study.

This review is to draw attention to some similarities between the traditional West African religious rituals and contemporary deliverance ministry/spiritual warfare practices.

High God-Supreme Creator

The concept of a Most High God was present in Africa along with the concept of lesser gods. Prayer was offered to the High God, but sacrifice was rare and reserved for the other gods and spirits of West African religions, including deceased ancestors. The traditional West African religions viewed the High God as parent to the lesser gods, who at times appeared to be mediators between man and the High God.

> Common to many African societies was belief in a High God, or Supreme Creator of the world and everything in it.... Early travelers were quick to note that Africans believed in a High god who transcended ritual relationships with humans. Describing religion on the Slave Coast, William Bosman, a Dutch factor, remarked that the Africans had an 'idea of the True God and ascribe to him the Attributes of Almighty, and Omnipresent.'... Occasionally individuals and communities did pray to the High God but sacrifice to him was rare; it was generally the other gods and the spirits of deceased ancestors who received the attention, since they had delegated to attend to 'the affairs of mankind.' Usually, in the traditional religions of West Africa the High God is the parent of the other and lesser gods, who are sometimes seen as mediators between man and God. (Raboteau, 1978, p.8 - 9)

The High God is not ignored in the West African tradition of religion, they were more traditionally concerned with the lesser gods and spirits.

> Though it would be a mistake to assume that the High God is forgotten or never appealed to, it is nevertheless a fundamental characteristic of West African religious life that the worshiper is most concerned with the lesser gods and spirits. (Raboteau, 1978, p.9)

The same could or may be said about the so-called modern day American based deliverance/spiritual warfare ministries, of all cultures.

Devils, Demons, and Spirit Possession

The lesser divinities or gods are numerous and are worshipped generally and or locally. Among some West African populations a group of gods known as pantheons are associated with phenomena, as well as natural forces. Sky pantheons, gods of the earth, water divinities and other nature spirits. These spirits or lesser divinities/gods may reside in or occupy inanimate as well as animate objects or substances. Some European travelers would accuse Africans of demonic worship.

> The lesser divinities or secondary gods are numerous. Some are worshipped generally, others only locally. Among some West African peoples there are pantheons, or groups of gods, associated with natural forces and phenomena. Sky pantheons include the god of thunder, lightning, and rainstorm. The gods of the earth govern fertility, and punish wickedness by sending smallpox and other virulent diseases. Water divinities dwell in or are identified with lakes, rivers, and the sea. Still other nature spirits may reside in trees, hills, winds, and animals. European travelers frequently identified African gods with demons or devils and accused Africans of devil worship. (Raboteau, 1978, p.9)

West Africans would refer to spirits by name, whom they believe to affect the affairs of men to do good or ill, by specific names.

> Africans refer to these spirits by various names: the Ashanti know them as *abosom*; the Ewe-speaking Fon of Dahomey name them *vodun;* the Ibo worship them as *alose;* and the Yoruba call them *orisha*. It is these gods who govern the forces of the world and affect the affairs of men for good or ill. The gods may be benevolent or malevolent as willful and arbitrary as humans. (Raboteau, 1978, p.10)

The spirit naming mindset is very similar to the contemporary mindset of deliverance ministry and spiritual warfare practitioners and

authors.   A review of Wink's *Naming The Powers,* Robeson's
Strongman's His Name What's His Game?, and Ing's *Spiritual Warfare*
would support this claim.

One of the traditional West African religious beliefs is that the
spirits impact the individual, the social, the national, and the cosmic
environment of mankind.

> "In the traditional religion of West Africa, the power of the gods
> and spirits was effectively present in the lives of men, for
> good or ill, on every level – environmental, individual, social,
> national, and cosmic. Aspects of reality seen as impersonal
> from a modern scientific viewpoint were not only personified
> but personalized, i.e., placed within the context of social
> relationships. The gods and men related to one another through
> the mediation of sacrifice, through the mechanism of
> divination, and through the phenomenon of spirit possession.
> (Raboteau, 1978, p. 11).

This traditional religion concept of West Africa, seems to be
consistent with what the deliverance ministry/spiritual warfare
contemporary viewpoint relative to the spirits impacting every aspect of
mankind's existence.

> The corporate spirits of IBM and Gulf Western are palpably real
> and striking different, as are the national spirits of the United
> States and Canada, or the congregational spirits ('angels' or
> 'demons' were actual entities, only they were not hovering in
> the air. They were incarnate in cellulose, or cement, or skin
> and bones, or an empire, or its mercenary armies. (Wink, 1986,
> p. 4 – 5)

Priests - Diviners and Devotees

The devotees acting as mediums of their gods on occasion may
become possessed or fall into an ecstatic trance or, "spirit possession", also
called being "mounted by the god."

The devotees have become mediums of their gods and upon the occasion of a ritual ceremony they may become possessed. In states of ecstatic trance, described by anthropologists of religion as 'spirit possession,' the *vodunsi* and *iyaworisha* dance out in mime the character of a god, becoming for a time the god's mouthpiece. Known as 'the horse of the god' or the 'owner of the god' or 'the one mounted by the god,' the ecstatic behavior of the possessed is highly stylized and controlled. (Raboteau, 1978, p.10 - 11)

There was/is a belief in the priests-diviners and others (devotees) who were considered experts in the areas of gods, spirits, spirit animation, and spirit possession, whom the gods spoke through, this would be known as "The Word of Knowledge," in contemporary deliverance settings.

Widely shared by diverse West African societies were several fundamental beliefs concerning the relationship of the divine to the human; belief in a transcendent, benevolent God, creator and ultimate source of providence; belief in a number of immanent gods, to whom people must sacrifice in order to make life propitious; belief in the power of spirits animating things in nature to affect the welfare of people; belief in priests and others who were expert in practical knowledge of the gods and spirits; belief in spirit possession, in which gods, through their devotees, spoke to men. (Raboteau, 1978, p.11 - 12)

The priests-diviners and/or devotees would lead and directed the ceremonies much in the same way that pastors, elders and deacons, in deliverance ministries conduct deliverance services today. The one exception may be the honoring of ancestors; or could it be that when we honor the founder(s) of a church, it is exactly what the West Africans were doing?

The various cults usually have priests and devotees who are active in their service to the gods. It is the role of the priest to offer worship and proper ritual sacrifice to the gods and to preside at periodic festivals honoring gods and ancestors. In addition, priests often serve as skilled diviners and herbalists. (Raboteau, 1978, p.10)

West African religious ritual similarities to what is occurring in the modern day deliverance ministry/spiritual warfare environment relative to worship leading is striking. The praise and worship activity that takes place in most deliverance ministry liturgical settings, bares a striking resemblance to what has occurred in African religious rituals.

> Perhaps the most obvious continuity between African and Afro-American religions is the style of performance in ritual action. Drumming, singing, and dancing are essential features of African and Afro-American liturgical expression and are crucial to the ceremonial possession of cult members by their gods. It is the rhythms of the drums which call upon the gods to manifest themselves in *condomble, shango, vaudou, and santeria.* (Raboteau, 1978, p.35)

Devotees had to go through a period of training that includes a symbolic death, learning a secret language, and are resurrected to a public cult initiation celebration.

> Devotees, known among the Yoruba and the Fon as *iyaworisha* and vodunsi, i.e., "wife of the orisha' or 'wife of the *vodun*' (through there [sic] are men devotees as well as women), are initiated into a cult over a more less lengthy period of training, which involves a novitiate in which the novice 'dies,' is instructed in the rites of the god, learns a secret language, and finally is 'resurrected,' to public celebration, as an initiate of the cult. (Raboteau, 1978, p.10)

It is interesting to note that in the Christian tradition you are baptized into the death of Jesus Christ, and resurrected in his life to become part of a church. To be a leader in a deliverance ministry/spiritual warfare environment in many cases you have to have been trained by an experienced deliverance ministry/spiritual warfare practitioner, learn and/or be anointed to speak in an unknown tongue, 'baptized in the spirit', as it is called by some. In some segments of the contemporary deliverance ministry or spiritual warfare arena, you would not be allowed to operate without a manifestation or a demonstration of the speaking in an unknown tongues, some may call it an anointing; or being baptized into or by the spirit; the Bible calls it a gift (I Corinthians 12).

Ancestral Worship – Familiar Spirits

Ancestral worship was part of the religious system of spirit awareness in the West African tradition.

> In addition to the gods, a powerful class of spirits in the world of traditional West African religions are the ancestors. ... It is believed that, as custodians of custom and law, the ancestors have the power to intervene is present affairs and, moreover, to grant fertility and health to their descendants, for whom they mediate with the gods.... It is commonly held that ancestors are born again in their descendants. A resemblance between a grandchild and his deceased grandfather, for example, is proof that the latter has been reincarnated in the former. West African parents turn to diviners to determine which ancestor's spirit has returned in their newborn child. (Raboteau, 1978, p.12)

In the contemporary deliverance ministry/spiritual warfare arena, the concept of the 'familiar spirit,' is similar to the ancestral spirit paradigm of West Africa. A definition of the term familiar spirit reveals a similarity to what the West Africans did in their ancestral worship.

> FAMILIAR SPIRIT. Divination by means of communication with the spirit of the dead (necromancy) was known and practiced in the ancient Near East 9cf. The Gilgamesh Epic, Tablet XII, where Gilgamesh conjured up the spirit of Enkidu in order to inquire about the state of the dead in the nether world. (Buttrick, et al., p. 237)

MacNutt discusses two theories regarding ancestral worship and familiar spirits. MacNutt also identifies an evangelical preference and differentiates between evil and departed sprits.

The last category of spirits we commonly encounter are named by ordinary, everyday, personal names like George or Susan. These are mysterious in origin. There are two very different theories explaining who they are.

The first theory is that they are simply masquerading as the souls of the dead, so as to excite people's curiosity about departed relatives, and hence to entice them into communicating with the dead through seances and other forbidden activities.

If this is true, then these evil spirits are to be treated like any other category of evil spirits and simply cast out. Most Christians of evangelical background prefer this understanding of familiar spirits.

The second theory is that these familiar spirits are truly the dead who are not at rest. In this case we should treat them not as evil spirits but as departed spirits who need prayer to commend them to Jesus, so that they might be set at rest and cease from wanderings. (MacNutt, 1995, p. 92 – 93)

The Sandfords' describe the familiar spirit as an agent of Satan assigned to a family for destruction. This description is consistent with the contemporary deliverance ministry/spiritual warfare definition   "A familiar spirit is Satan's 'angel' assigned to a family to use unredeemed areas in its history and whatever demons are available to 'steal, and kill, and destroy' family members (John 10:10)" (Sanford and Sanford, 1992, p.55).

This review has examined some of the phenomenon and similarities that can be detected relative to traditional West African religious rituals and contemporary deliverance ministry. And I have come to the conclusion that West African religious rituals has had some impact on the contemporary deliverance ministry arena, particularly relative to the phenomenon of possession.

> The phenomenon of possession is the climax of the service in every one of the cults we have noted. Whether the possessing spirit is Shango in *candomble,* an ancestor in the Convince cult, a spirit in Cumina, or the Holy Spirit in the Shouters' service, the ritual context in which possession occurs and the physiological behavior of the possessed are strikingly uniform. (Raboteau, 1978, p.36)

There are other African religious ritual deliverance-like behavior similarities that could be discussed if time, space and primary focus would permit. To name a few: revelatory magic and channeling, choreography and ritual dancing and shouting and praise and worship forms. As stated earlier in this section, African religious ritual practices have had some impact on the Pentecostal/Charismatic movement. This movement in return has impacted contemporary deliverance ministry/spiritual warfare practices. Many Africans practice Christianity alongside their traditional religions. An investigation of other cultures' religious ritual practices could yield some deliverance-like patterns and behaviors.

Religious and Other Paranormal Beliefs in the United States

In my opinion it would be of some benefit to review some religious and paranormal beliefs that may be relevant to this treatise/study. Information will be extrapolated from a study titled "Believe It Or Not: Religious and Other Paranormal Beliefs in the United States." It appeared in the March 2003 publication of the; *Journal for the Scientific Study of Religion;* my strategy will be to provide a brief overview of the article, and to select some of the questions and responses that may be germane to this treatise/study.

The author outlines the purpose of the study and some areas of disagreement.

> American scholars often distinguish between religious and classic paranormal beliefs. The former are central to traditional Christian doctrine, such as the belief in heaven and hell, the devil, and creationism, and the latter commonly

associated with the supernatural or occult, such as the belief in ESP, reincarnation, psychic healing, and UFOs. Both sets of beliefs are paranormal because they 'transcend the explanatory power of mainstream science' (Gray 1991:7), but social scientists disagree over the extent to which the two belief structures intersect. They also disagree over the social correlates of paranormal beliefs, especially classic paranormal beliefs. This study employs data from a recent nationwide random sample general population survey to catalog the social correlates of paranormal beliefs and to examine the relationships between religious and classic paranormal beliefs. The comprehensive nature of the survey sample, combined with the unusually rich array of paranormal questions, afford a unique opportunity to investigate the nature of paranormal beliefs structures in the contemporary United States. (Rice, 2003, p. 95)

The author also identifies the theory that defines this type of research.

Deprivation theory serves as the foundation for much of the research examining the social correlates of religious and classic paranormal beliefs. The theory maintains that paranormal beliefs provide people with the means to cope with the psychological and physical strain of disadvantaged social and economic status (Glock and Stark 1965; Stark and Bainbridge 1980). Thus, belief in the paranormal should be higher among marginal social groups, such as minorities and the poor. The studies examining the correlates of traditional religious beliefs present a fairly uniform set of conclusions that are, for the most part, consistent with the deprivation theory... (Rice, 2003, p. 95)

The author shares the two primary hypotheses that scholars seem to feel surfaced after examination.

Scholars who have examined the interrelationships between religious and classic paranormal beliefs have been guided by two hypothesis. One holds that there should be an inverse relationship between the two belief structures; that is, most people who believe in one type of paranormalism will not believe in the other. For some researchers, this hypothesis is based on the idea that classic paranormalism functions as a set of substitute beliefs for people who are outside mainstream religions (Emmons and Sobal 1981). For others, the hypothesis rests on the notion that lay Christians will reject classic paranormal beliefs because their church hierarchies do not endorse them (Goode 2000b; Sparks 2001). Either way, the result should be a negative correlation between the belief in religious and classic paranormal phenomena.

The second hypothesis takes the opposite view, contending that people who believe in one type of paranormal phenomena will also tend to believe in the other. To proponents of this position, it is a small step to move from believing in the devil and angels to believing in ghosts and aliens; both 'affirm the existence of realities beyond the mundane existence of everyday life' and both lie outside accepted science (Wuthnow 1978:71). (Rice, 2003, p. 96)

The author also articulates that investigations have produced some contradictory/conflicting outcomes. "The empirical work testing these rival hypotheses has produced contradictory results. Several scholars find an inverse relationship between the belief in certain religious and classic paranormal phenomena..." (Rice, 2003, p. 97)

Extrapolated Questions and Answers
From Table 1 Paranormal Questions and Frequencies

Core Paranormal Questions

Religious Paranormal Beliefs
  1. **Do you believe that after people die, some souls go to Heaven and others go to Hell?**
     Believe 63.4%   Don't Believe 24.6%
     Not sure/No Answer 12.0%

2. Do you believe that people on this Earth are sometimes possessed by the Devil?
Believe 58.6%   Don't Believe 29.7%
Not sure/No Answer 11.7%

3. Do you believe that God answers prayers?
Believe 83.1%   Don't Believe 9.8%
Not sure/No Answer 7.1%

Classic Paranormal Beliefs

6. Do you believe that extraterrestrial beings have visited Earth at some time in the past?
Believe 35.2%   Don't Believe 39.6%
Not sure/No Answer 25.2%

7. Do you believe in ghosts, that is, that spirits of dead people can came back in certain places and situations
Believe 42.1%   Don't Believe 46.8%
Not sure/No Answer 11.0%

8. Do you believe in psychic or spiritual healing, that is, the power of the human mind to heal the human body?
Believe 58.6%   Don't Believe 29.7%
Not sure/No Answer 11.7%

Other Paranormal Questions
Paranormal Beliefs

11. Which one of these statements comes closest to your belief about God; 1) There is a God; 2) There is a spirit or life force; 3) I don't believe there is any kind of spirit, God, or life force?
God 80.6%   Spirit/Life Force 14.5
Neither 3.8%   Don't know/No Answer 1.1%

12. Which do you think is a more likely explanation for the origin of human life on Earth—The Biblical account of creation or Darwinian evolution?
Biblical Account 55.8%   Evolution 28.5%
Both 6.1%   Neither/No Opinion 9.5%

Paranormal Experiences

16. Have you personally ever experienced having an Illness cured by prayer?
Yes 33.6%   No 63.1%
Not Sure/No Answer 3.3%

17. Have you personally ever used the power of your mind to heal your own body?
Yes 27.1%   No 69.9%
Not Sure/No Answer 3.0%
(Rice, 2003, p.98)

Extrapolated Questions and Answers Review

From the seventeen original questions in Table 1, (Paranormal Questions and Frequencies) in my opinion, ten have topics that are more germane to this process. The review relative to Questions One, Two, and Three under "Core Paranormal Questions – Religious Paranormal Beliefs" reveal that 63.4% of the respondents believe that some souls go to Heaven or Hell, 58.6 % of the respondents believe that people are sometimes possessed by the Devil, and 83.1% of the respondents believe that God answers prayer. From my perspective this is significant relative to the nature of this treatise/study especially the responses to Questions Two and Three that broach the issues of devil possession and God answering prayers.

Under "Core Paranormal Questions, Classic Paranormal Beliefs" the responses to Questions Six, Seven, and Eight; indicate that 35.2% of the respondents believe in extraterrestrial visitation, 42.1% of the respondents believe that the spirits of the dead come back; and 58.6% of the respondents believe in psychic or spiritual healing. This is also significant relative to this study, especially the responses to Questions Seven and Eight, ghosts and healing.

Under "Other Paranormal Questions – Paranormal Beliefs": the responses to Questions Eleven indicate that 80.6% of the respondents believe in God, and 14.5% believe in a Spirit/Life Force. Question Twelve reveals that 55.8% of the respondents believe the Biblical account of life on Earth. This is significant in the contrast of a spiritualistic or materialistic world view mindset in the United States.

Under "Other Paranormal Questions – Paranormal Experiences", the respondents to Question Sixteen indicate that 33.6% have experienced being cured by prayer and 63.1% have not experienced being cured by prayer. I find the response to Question Sixteen significant in light of the responses to Question Three. The difference between beliefs and experiences relative to prayer is interesting. Relative to Question Seventeen the respondents indicated that 27.1% of them used the power of the mind to heal their own bodies, 69.9% indicated they had not used the power of their mind for healing.

In my opinion, this review has provided some valuable insights relative to religious and other paranormal beliefs, from a cross section of cultures, in the United States. This input has augmented the information base relative to the focus of this treatise/study. I recommend a reading of the study for a more complete and thorough understanding of the study and all of the ramifications of the research

Prayer

This treatise/study focus is on a ministry event to determine whether or not impact in the form of reaction(s) and behavior(s) will occur when a specific format of Deliverance Prayer is prayed for those seeking deliverance. This section of the Theory/Literature Review will focus on the topic of prayer and some activities that are connected to the activity of prayer. The prayer selected as the specific prayer format for this treatise/study, will be a part of this section's review.

As the controversy rages relative to possession, demonization, oppression, affliction, internal or external; one thing seems to be consistent in addressing the issue no matter the theology, that is prayer is essential and it works. There seems to be agreement that there is power in prayer in general and specifically Deliverance Prayer that impacts the demons relative to possession, deliverance, and exorcising the demonic realm.

Walter Wink believed prayer is indispensable in engaging the powers. He also made a powerful statement about prayer not being a private act.

> Those who pray do so not because they believe certain intellectual propositions about the value of prayer, but simply because the struggle to be human in the face of superhuman Powers requires it. The act of praying is itself one of the indispensable means by which we engage the Powers. It is, in fact, that engagement at its most fundamental level, where their secret spell over us is broken and we are reestablished in a bit more of that freedom which is our birthright and potential.

> Prayer is never a private act. It may be the interior battlefield where the decisive victory is first won, before engagement in the outer world is even attempted. If we have not undergone that inner liberation, whereby the individual strands of the nets in which we are caught are severed, one by one, our activism may merely reflect one or another counter ideology of some counter-Power. We may simply be caught up in a new collective passion, and fail to discover the transcendent possibilities of God pressing for realization here and now. Unprotected by prayer, our social activism runs the danger of becoming self-justifying good works, as our inner resources atrophy, the wells of love run dry, and we are slowly changed into the likeness of the Beast. (Wink, 1992, p. 297 – 298)

Some authors distinguish between prayer and a command for the demons or evil spirits to leave.

What is the basic form of deliverance prayer?... The first
thing to realize when we are performing a deliverance is that
deliverance prayer is different from prayer for healing. In
fact, it is not prayer at all, it is a *command*. And it is directed
not to God, as prayer is, but to an evil spirit, ordering it to get
out. This command is backed up by God's authority, in the
name of Jesus Christ. Paul for instance, cast out the
soothsaying spirit from the slave girl who kept pestering him:
'She kept this up for many days. Finally Paul became so
troubled that he turned around and said to the spirit, 'In the
name of Jesus Christ I command you to come out of her!' At
that moment the spirit left her. Acts 16:18' Healing prayer,
on the other hand, is directed to God. We certainly do not
command God to do anything; we only ask Him – in this case
to heal. (MacNutt, 1995, p. 167)

Kraft believes that to engage in deliverance ministry, prayer is
essential, he describes it as ministering freedom.

My point is, there is a lot of work to do with today's
equivalent of "the lost sheep of the house of Israel " (Mt.
15:24; 10:6). And many of God's people need to learn how to
minister freedom to them, if the church is to become what
Jesus intended it to be.

To move into this ministry, here are steps I, and those who work
with me, have been following: 1. We began by praying, letting
God know we were open to whatever he chose to bring our
way. We prayed for opportunities to engage in Jesus
freeing ministry, and for the necessary guidance, authority,
and power. (Kraft, 1992, p. 29)

Mitchell discusses an ancient prayer of exorcism that binds
the spirits for eternity. feel certain that when spirits are bound
in Christ's name and sent away 'to the place prepared for
them' (in the words of an ancient prayer of exorcism) they go
to a place where they are bound to remain forever. (Mitchell,
1999, p.127)

Monroe articulates that mankind has the power to be delivered from Satan's dominion through prayer based on the word of God.

> Satan is the prince of darkness, and he became the god of this world when he successfully tempted Adam and Eve to reject God's ways. Yet through Christ, we have been delivered from satan's, dominion, out of the realm of darkness. That is why, even though we continue to live in a fallen world, we do not belong to it, We belong to God's Kingdom. Power in prayer is not based on emotions, feelings, or the theories of men, but upon the Word of God. (Monroe, 2002, p. 55 - 57)

Chavda suggest that fasting should be added to prayer when engaging in spiritual warfare. This author also suggests the power of group prayer and fasting for greater victories.

> The key to defeating dark strongholds is twofold. First we must tap the *power* of the Spirit through the combination of prayer and fasting; and second, we will overcome in the largest battles in this generation only when we pray and fast *together* and unleash the incredible power of the Body of Christ on its knees. ... An unavoidable part of the works of Jesus begins with prayer and fasting because these were the first works of Jesus in His mission to destroy the works of the enemy. (Chavda, 1998, p. 74)

According to Zuendel, Blumhardt viewed prayer as one of the only two acceptable pure weapons against "personalities of darkness."

> For Blumhardt, the only acceptable tools were the 'pure weapons of prayer and the word of God.' The building up of the church in Mottlingen did not begin with preaching but, as he put it, with struggle, prayer, and finally, victory over 'personalities of darkness.' (Zuendel, 2000, p. xvii)

Prayer is the most powerful tool against the powers of darkness in the act of deliverance ministry. Jesus Christ prayed during periods of spiritual deliverance ministry. If the spiritual warfare was intense he would fast, Matt 4:1 – 11. Jesus Christ pointed out in Matthew 17: 17 –

21, the focus is on verse 21, that some demons cannot be cast out unless you pray and fast. "Then came the disciples to Jesus apart, and said, Why could not we cast him out? ... Howbeit this kind goeth not out but by prayer and fasting" (Matt 17:19, 21, KJV).

There are three areas I need to draw attention to before I leave the prayer section of the Theory/Literature Review chapter; they are: "The Word of Knowledge," "Slain in the Spirit," and "Laying on of Hands." Any one of these could occur during deliverance prayer. Two of the three, "The Word of Knowledge" and "Slain in the Spirit' are considered phenomenon. They have been defined in Appendix F.

The Word of Knowledge

The word of knowledge according to Scripture is a gift of the Holy Spirit "Now concerning spiritual gifts, brethren, I do not want you to be ignorant: ...For to one is given the word of wisdom through the Spirit, to another the word of knowledge through the same Spirit" (I Corinthians. 12:1, 8, NKJ).

This is a supernatural gift that comes from the Holy Spirit and reveals certain aspects of the mind of God, according to Kenneth E. Hagin

> Notice that this gift is called "the word of knowledge." It is not "the gift of knowledge' There is no such thing as a spiritual gift of knowledge. There is however, a spiritual gift, called the word of knowledge. The word of knowledge is the *supernatural revelation by the Holy Spirit of certain facts in the mind of God.*
>
> God is all-knowing. He knows everything. But He doesn't reveal everything He knows to man. He just gives him a word or a part of what He knows. A word is a fragmentary part of a sentence, so a word of knowledge would simply be a fragmentary part of the entire knowledge or counsel of God. God is all-knowing. He has all knowledge. But he doesn't impart all of His knowledge to us. He imparts a word of

knowledge to us – just what He wants us to know at a given time.

This word of knowledge is a supernatural manifestation as are all of these gifts of the Spirit. None of them are natural gifts; they are all supernatural gifts. Since one of them is supernatural, they all are supernatural. If one of them were natural, then all of them would be natural (Hagin, 1991, p. 75).

Some may attempt to argue that the word of knowledge is a natural thought process, that this gift is not supernatural.

There are those who say that this gift of the Spirit – the word of knowledge – refers to natural knowledge. If that were true, then all the gifts of the Spirit, would be natural, not supernatural. If that were true, for example, then the gifts of healings would not be supernatural healing, but simply healing through what people have learned and achieved through medical science. (Hagin, 1991, p. 75)

I realize that this gift can be dramatized or perpetrated, as in many things of the Spirit. However, I agree with the author relative to the gift called "The Word Of Knowledge."

Slain in the Spirit

There is definitely some serious controversy around the phenomena known as Slain in the Spirit or "Falling under the Power."

In this chapter we are talking about what is commonly called "falling under the power." I must confess that I am not a happy writer. I don't want to write about true and false in the same area since even the idea of "true" falling offends my sense of propriety and probably my pride (which God has determined to resist ahead of time – I Peter 5:5). However, to follow the inner mandate and to handle this book with integrity, falling as a religious and spiritual phenomenon, like many other things, must be divided into true and false. Indeed, so influential writer a figure as John Wimber said this, there's no

place in the Bible where people were lined up and Jesus or Paul
or anyone else went along and bopped them on the head and
watched them go down, and someone else ran along behind.
Can you picture Peter and James –"Hold it, hold it, hold it!" –
running along behind trying to catch them, and so the model
we're seeing, either on stage or on television, is totally
different from anything that's in Scripture. (Foster, 2001,
p. 287)

Foster quotes Keith M. Bailey's observations which points out that
you cannot find the phenomena in the Bible, the way we see it today.

The expressions 'falling under the power' and slain in the
Spirit" are non-biblical. They do not describe the experiences
of falling found in Scripture. In both the Old and New
Testaments incidents are found where godly people were
overcome by the extraordinary presence of God. The biblical
manifestations show little if any similarity to the modern falling
experiences. (Foster, 2001, p. 293)

Foster points out examples from the Bible, such as, Deuteronomy
9:18; Ezra 9:5; John 18:4-6; and Acts 9:3-6.

This phenomenon has been characterized today as a Charismatic or
Pentecostal movement. However, there were signs of this phenomena
documented as early as 1801, where Baptists, Methodist and
Presbyterians were present.

At Cane Ridge in Bourbon County, Kentucky in 1801, at the
most famous of America's camp meetings, there were many
manifestations. In crowds estimated to be as large as 20,000,
the people fell by the hundreds. Set in a context of
Presbyterianism, eventually the camp meeting embraced the
Baptists and Methodists as well. (Foster, 2001, p. 291)

Some prominent ministers have had experience with this phenomenon.

Although I prayed with boldness, I wasn't sure what to do next. So, I waited. It seemed as though time stood still at that moment. Not a sound could be heard. I didn't know what was happening, but I wasn't about to open my eyes. I just knelt there, eyes closed, and kept praying.

Suddenly there was a loud noise and another. It startled me and I opened my eyes to see what had happened. As I looked around I saw the man, his wife, and daughter all lying on the floor. The Spirit of God had descended with such power that the man and his family fell backward to the floor. (Hinn, 1995, p. 210 -211)

Another noted minister, Kenneth E. Hagin recounts some experiences and identifies some scriptures to support this manifestation.

Why do people fall under the power of God? When the natural comes into contact with the supernatural – something has to give. Church history records that in every great move of God's power and Spirit -- people fell. Half the New Testament is written by Paul, a fellow who fell under the power. (Hagin, 1981, p. 2)

Hagin has realized this phenomenon on several occasions with large groups, and in one- on-one situations.

I remember one time I was preaching at Christ for the Nations and we had a healing line. I was laying hands on people when I saw the glory cloud coming in, enveloping them. I stepped up in front of the pulpit on the platform and noticed all the people had their eyes shut. As the cloud rolled in, I just waved my hand and every one of them went down like dominos. Several times that has happened to me. (Hagin, 1981, p. 18)

She said, "Well, I'm ready to believe it.' I saw that she was ready. I reached my hand out and barely brushed her forehead. The power of God went into her and she fell backwards right on the floor. (Hagin, 1981, p.16)

Hagin cites several scriptural references: John 18:1 – 6, Matthew 28: 1 - 4, Matthew 17: 6, Acts 9:4, Acts 26:14, Ezekiel 1:28; 2:1 - 2. Many would challenge these scriptures based on semantics, and no solid biblical example of it happening, the same exact way it is happening today.

One of the authors that I feel has done some extensive research concerning the phenomenon of "Slaying or Slain in the Spirit' or what is sometimes called " Resting in the Spirit,' is Francis MacNutt, in his book, *The Power to Heal.* In Chapter Fifteen, "Resting in the Spirit:" he touches on the experience of others as well as personal experiences including some history; he also offers some areas of caution.

Experiences of others

I talked to one priest who went to a Kathryn Kuhlman meeting in Pittsburgh and was so sensitive to this power that he couldn't get near her but repeatedly fell down in the aisle as he tried to approach the platform. It sounded strange to me (MacNutt, 1977, p. 189)

Personal experiences

But then several people I prayed for experienced this and proceeded to rest for a considerable time. Afterwards, they told me of some deep spiritual experience they had while in that state. (MacNutt, 1977, p. 192)

Because most people who experience this phenomenon report that they are more alive than ever interiorly, I prefer not to speak of it as being 'slain in the Spirit," which only refers to something external, a body falling to the ground. It's quite the opposite of being "slain'; it's more like too much life for the body to bear. So I'm for getting rid of the word "slain' which connotes violence. (MacNutt, 1977, p. 204)

Some history

> Observe the following accompaniments to Wesley's preaching, about which he was happy at Limerick in 1762, 'Many more were brought to the birth.
>
> All were in floods of tears, cried, prayed, roared aloud, all of them lying on the ground.' At Newcastle in 1772, 'An eminent backslider came into my mind, and I broke off abruptly... 'Is James Watson here? If he be, thy power.' Down dropped James Watson like a stone.' At Coleford in 1784, "When I began to pray, the flame broke out. Many   cried aloud, many sank to the ground, many trembled exceedingly.' (MacNutt, 1977, p. 198 – 199)

Some cautions

> Clearly, in all this, there can be problems, principally because it appears so sensational and people understand it so little. It's something like the gift of tongues when it was quite new; people are impressed because it is so different, so sensation-seeking can easily take over. Hopefully, when resting in the Spirit is better known, its spiritual purpose will become central, and it will no longer cause astonishment. But the answer to most of these problems is not suppression. (MacNutt, 1977, p. 215 – 216)

I recommend Foster and MacNutt for contrasting perspectives on this phenomenon.

The position I take regarding biblical phenomenon, is that what happened on Pentecost with the apostles never had happened before that historical event. Many scholars believe that the book of Acts is not finished. Perhaps many of these occurrences and/or phenomenon documented in modern day history will be part of the book's completion. Jesus Christ said, "Verily, verily, I say unto you, He that believeth on me, the works that I do shall he do also; and greater works than these shall he do; because I go unto my Father" (John 14:12, KJV). The reader will have to decide for him or herself.

Laying on of Hands

This activity is one that is biblically supported relative to healing and deliverance.

There are those who contend that Jesus never laid hands on anyone during deliverance. There are at least two instances that indicate otherwise. One is the healing of Peter's mother-in-law. In Luke 4:39 we are told that Jesus 'rebuked the fever". He treated the fever as a personality. This indicates that the fever was demonic. The parallel account in Matt. 8:15 says, "And he *touched* her hand, and the fever left her." A second instance of touching or laying hands on a person for deliverance is the case of the woman who was bowed together by a spirit of infirmity.

And, behold, there was a woman which had a spirit of infirmity eighteen years, and was bowed together, and could in no wise lift up herself. And when Jesus saw her, he called her to him, and said unto her, Woman, thou art loosed from thine infirmity. AND HE LAID HIS HANDS ON HER: and immediately she was made straight, and glorified God. Luke 13:11-13 (Hammond & Hammond, p. 78)

Laying on of hands is not mandatory or prohibited relative to the Word of God (*The Bible*), but it is considered a sign of believers. 'They shall take up serpents; and if they drink any deadly thing, it shall not hurt them; they shall lay hands on the sick, and they shall recover.' (Mark 16:18, KJV)

My philosophy would be very close to how Whyte approaches this issue relative to deliverance.

I usually begin deliverance sessions by praying for that person without laying my hands on them. If the sufferer begins to show signs of distress, I then use the laying on of hands to bring the force of the Holy Spirit to bear upon him. (Whyte, 1989, p. 170)

The considerable focus given to: "The Word of Knowledge," "Slain in the Spirit," and "Laying on of Hands" was necessary because these may become part of the Ministry Research Event, as a result of this prayer, but are not the focus of my research. Therefore, I have attempted to expose the reader, not thoroughly inform them on these subjects. The attempt at brevity was by design; I personally do not have a theological conflict with any of these areas.

Prayer Selection

I think it is important to state at this point that faith in God has to be the basis from which deliverance ministry and spiritual warfare are connected. There are no 'magic formulas,' success in prayer and warfare is not predicated on certain words but a relationship with God and faith in His Word. There are authors who would agree with this position.

> Wearing armor and praying the Word of God is not some sort of "magic formula." Success is not guaranteed if certain words are spoken concerning a specific situation. Prayer and warfare must be solidly based upon faith in God and a relationship with the God whose Word we declare. The Apostle John writes: "Dear friends, if our hearts do not condemn us, we have confidence before God and receive from him anything we ask, because we obey his commands and do what pleases him" (I John 3:21-22). (Sherrer and Garlock, 1992, p.21)

I also must state that I truly believe that when faith in the Word of God is connected to a relationship with The Father, Son, and The Holy Spirit, and if what is prayed for falls into the context of His Will and plan; I believe that impact in the form of reaction(s) and behavior(s) will manifest.

I selected the prayer from Dr. L. David Mitchell's book, *Liberty in Jesus*, because of the content, brevity, and simplicity. Reading the book gave some great insights into the author's skill and anointing in the field of deliverance, as well as his education, longevity, experience and success in the deliverance arena.

I would have to say that what made this decision final for me is that I met Dr. Mitchell and observed his deliverance methodology during a seminar. I had the opportunity to discuss deliverance ministry and spiritual warfare with him. His insight relative to how demons operate is informative, interesting, and balanced from my perspective. Dr. Mitchell's prayer is outlined in the Methodology section of this study. I feel at this point, a short bio on Dr. Mitchell would be appropriate.

> Prior to training for the Anglican ministry at Wells Theological College, David Mitchell qualified and practiced as a Chartered Accountant in England. Ordained in 1961, he worked in rural and city parishes. In 1967, in Canada, he began ten years bi-vocational mission in the world of business. Then followed several years of extensive counselling [sic], conducting evangelistic and renewal missions, and retreats, and producing a series of spiritual development exercises. As a Senior Pastor with the Christian & Missionary Alliance in Canada, he served on the Board of Directors. David Mitchell today ministers across denominational boundaries. His Doctor of Ministry dissertation for Canadian Theological Seminary was on training for deliverance ministry. (Mitchell, 1999, back cover)

Theory of Deliverance – My Perspective

A great deal of theory has been discussed up until this point relative to spiritual warfare and demonic deliverance. My position is that spiritual warfare (demonic deliverance) is one of the three major assignments that Jesus Christ has instructed the Church/body of believers/disciples to do: preach the gospel, cast out demons and heal the sick.

> And He said to them, "Go into all the world and preach the gospel to every creature. He who believes and is baptized will be saved; but he who does not believe will be condemned. And these signs will follow those who believe: In My name they will cast out demons; they will speak with new tongues; they will take up serpents; and if they drink anything deadly, it will by no means hurt them; they will lay

hands on the sick, and they will recover." (Mark 16:15-18, NKJ)

This text requires some clarification.

> The original Gospel ended with Mark 16:8. Yet there are scholars who argue strongly for a lost ending (a final codex page that became detached?), contending that Mark would surely have narrated the appearance in Galilee promised in 16:7 (as does Matt 28:16 – 20). (Brown, 1997, p.148)

I believe that Satan and demons exist and that believers in the Christian context can be possessed, demonized, oppressed, obsessed and depressed by the Satanic – demonic realm.   And, I believe that deliverance ministry/spiritual warfare is the means to confront the issue of casting out demons through powerful deliverance command prayers.

Chapter Three
Methodology

Research Strategy

This was a qualitative experimental research study using random sampling observation of the participants with an open-ended question to the participants.

Based on the two major categories – quantitative and qualitative; qualitative seems to be more suitable to this kind of study, in my opinion, for the following reasons:

1. Qualitative research uses the natural setting as the direct source of data and the researcher as the key instrument. Qualitative researchers go to the particular setting under study because they are concerned with context.
2. Qualitative research is descriptive.
3. Qualitative researchers are concerned with process rather than simply with outcomes or products.
4. Qualitative researchers tend to analyze their data inductively.
5. Meaning is of essential concern to the qualitative approach. Researchers who use this approach are interested in the ways people make sense out of their lives. In other words, qualitative researchers are concerned with what are called participant perspectives. (Slavin, 1992, p. 66 – 68)

Experimental, random sampling and participant observation have been defined in the definition section. The leaning is toward qualitative but elements of the quantitative approach are evident; you could say a modified combination of both approaches.

I propose to participate in a deliverance prayer meeting and pray for at least five people at this meeting. I will use a deliverance prayer from the L. Mitchell book, *Liberty in Jesus*, "A form of deliverance command: 'In the Name of the Lord Jesus Christ, and by the power of his Precious Blood, I bind every spirit of... and command you to leave me (or ... This child of God), and go to the place prepared for you, harming nobody, now. AMEN" (Mitchell, 1999, p. 180).

I propose to use this command verbatim inserting the word evil after "spirit of . . . " and used the statement "This child of God." The external reaction(s) and behavior(s) will be recorded. Each participant will be invited to respond to the question, "What did you experience?" The participants will be selected randomly by the Deliverance Prayer Session Leader, an Apostle, from a group of people who attend churches other than the one I pastor. The location has been secured and permission from participants has been obtained. This was achieved by announcing the event four consecutive weeks prior, relative to participation. The Apostle who oversees the meeting has given his verbal permission. The Apostle has been conducting inner healing/deliverance and spiritual warfare meetings at this location every Friday for over thirteen years.

Individuals attending these meetings will have the option to participate or decline; permission will be verbal. The verbal permission scenario developed as a result of my relationship with the session leader, the Apostle and my involvement with the Friday night inner healing and deliverance ministry/spiritual warfare sessions. I have been involved in these sessions for over fifteen months on a weekly basis prior to this study. Credibility with the session leader and, my reputation that grew among the participants led to the level of trust that allowed for verbal consent or decline relative to this study.

Deliverance meetings are conducted in many formats. The format for this session is anticipated to be as it has been for the last fifteen months, that I have observed and participated. There is usually a two or two and a half-hour inner healing/deliverance message. After the message the session leader identifies the intercessors or Deliverance Prayer warriors to come before the audience/participants; the prayer warriors stand facing the group.

There will be at least four other individuals praying during this session using a different deliverance prayer format. Those engaged as deliverance intercessors/ or deliverance prayer warriors will line up facing the group, and those interested in being prayed for will be sent to the first/next available intercessor/deliverance prayer warrior. Because some people fall, or experience what some call the phenomenon "Slain in the Spirit;" people called catchers are placed behind the person being prayed for to prevent injury. Some intercessors may lay hands on the person they are praying for, and some do not. I tend to use both techniques and/or approaches.

Along with the phenomenon known as "Falling or Slain in the Spirit" there is the potential of receiving the gift of the Holy Spirit called, "the Word of Knowledge." Neither of these events can be controlled, planned, predicted or prevented. I should mention another phenomenon that could occur, that I have not covered, "Speaking in Tongues." This phenomenon is manifested in the form of someone speaking in a divine language or a language they have not previous learned. This phenomenon was not reviewed because of the intensity of the controversy surrounding this issue would require research equal to the scope of this entire treatise/study. The Bible calls this phenomenon a gift, in first Corinthians the twelfth chapter. There will be four experienced observers/recorders involved in this observation/study process, in addition to myself; they will have a background in deliverance ministry. The observers will record what they see, using the "Participant Observation – Random Sampling Observation Tool," designed for this study (see page 84).

Participant Observation – Random Sampling Tool
Deliverance Prayer Survey Observation

Observer's Name:

Gender of Participant: Female_____Male _____

Observation:_____

Eye activity_____

Coughing/Choking_____

Vomiting_____

Throwing up Phlegm_____

Falling to the Floor_____

Noises:_____

Other Body Movements:_____

Other Observations:_____

One of the observers will attempt to come to me between intercessions and record my observation(s). If this is not feasible it will be discontinued. The same observer will ask the participant; "What did you experience?" The annotated observed reaction(s), behavior(s), and the responses to the, " What did you experience?" question, will be categorized and compared for each person prayed for. The data will be used to respond to the question relative to impact. Each impact will be categorized based on the types of manifestations during the prayer. The information from this research will be analyzed in light of my journey relative to deliverance ministry/spiritual warfare. The language in this chapter has a pre event tense because it describes the proposed activities; in my opinion this maintains the authenticity of the process.

Credentials of Observers

Freddie
Education: BA, Social Studies, Secondary Teaching Certificate – Social Studies MA, Education Administration
Years in Occupation: 23 – Educator
Years in Church: 15
Years in Deliverance Ministry: 5

Edna
Education: BA, Management, Secondary Teaching Certificate – Social Studies
Years in Occupation: 13 – Educator
Years in Church: 15
Years in Deliverance Ministry: 5

Elder Steve
Education: 2 years college, Commercial Arts Major
Years in Occupation: 3 – Manager, Home Building Supplies
Years in Church: 13
Years in Deliverance Ministry: 13, Elder 4 years

Denise
Education: BS, Mathematics and Business Administration, Secondary
Teaching Certificate Master in the Art of Teaching
Years in Occupation: 12 – Educator
Years in Church: 4
Years in Deliverance Ministry: 2.5

Last names are not revealed to protect the privacy of the observers.
Survey participants will be identified by number in order of observation
and by gender. The observation survey tool and the observations will be
presented exactly as recorded by the particular observer, and in order as
they appear on the observer's credential page(s). The survey instrument
itself is a one-page instrument to insure that the observer would have
adequate space to comment. To save space for the purpose of this
presentation there will be two survey observation outcomes per page, and
an Observation Tool Consolidation Chart, for a more concise
presentation of the data. The surveys and the participant interview
question response forms can be reviewed in the appendix section.

Chapter Four
Ministry Research Event

Event Description – Context

The Ministry Research Event took place on November 8, 2002, 7:30 p.m. through 12:00 a.m. The intercessors came together at 7:15 p.m. for prayer led by the Apostle, the session leader. The meeting began with prayer and a praise and worship session. All first time visitors were asked to stand and introduce themselves and give their church affiliation, if any. At that point, the Apostle gave a Word of Knowledge to the first time visitors, based on how he felt the Holy Spirit was leading him. Tithes/offerings, and announcements were next on the agenda. After that, the Apostle/Session Leader explained the Ministry Research Event that would occur that evening. The Session Leader indicated that he had given his prior approval and consent, but anyone who did not want to be a part of the observation could decline being prayed for by Dr. Ernest Maddox. The Session Leader proceeded with the message for this session.

There was a two and a half-hour message on inner healing and deliverance ministry/spiritual warfare. The group was cross gender, and multi-cultural, with ages ranging from children to senior citizens. The youngest children were sent to a youth program during the session, if parents chose that option. The environment is nontraditional, not "churchy;" it is casual, relaxed, but orderly.

The prayer process began immediately after the question and answer session following the message. I was among about ten other Deliverance Prayer Intercessors that were asked to come up and face the body. The Apostle and the Pastor under him prayed for the Deliverance Prayer Intercessors and placed olive oil on our foreheads and hands (anointing with oil). In this group of Deliverance Intercessors are ordained

individuals as well as lay persons. The ordained intercessors included
the Apostle, his wife, the Prophetess, an Evangelist, the Pastor, Teachers,
Elders, and Missionaries. The four observers were in place and had been
present since 7:15 p.m. Their responsibility was to observe, not pray for
anyone or be prayed for at this session. I conducted a short briefing
meeting before the session began.

The Apostle announced that prayer would begin and anyone
wanting to be prayed for should come forward. A line then formed in the
center aisle of the church, which has rows of movable chairs, and is set
up in a lecture hall format. The Apostle reminded everyone about the
Ministry Research Event, and that they could decline participating by
letting him know that they did not want to be prayed for by Dr. Maddox.
This option was a provision for the Ministry Event. Normally the person
assigned to you by the Session Leader, once you have presented yourself
for prayer would pray for you. The Apostle began to send people to the
Deliverance Prayer intercessors.

The assignments were random, the Session Leader made the
decision; sending participants to the next available intercessor. I used the
prayer format outlined in the Methodology Chapter. I prayed, that I and
the ones I would be praying for, be covered in the Blood of Jesus Christ
during the Deliverance Prayer intercession process.

Event Dynamics

First of all, I have to say that the energy level in the room seemed to
be very high and once prayer began there was constant and continuous
activity. There was noise of prayer, crying, praising, screaming,
shouting, and chairs being moved to make room. The room is not very
large and that evening, there were about 110 people present.

As I began to pray for the first person that was sent to me, I realized
that I would not be able to make any accurate observations without
taking time to write them down between intercessions. The observer
that was to interview me did not have time to record their observations,
interview the participant and then record my observations. As a result my
observations are not a part of the official data gathering process, relative

to what happened in some detail with the person I was interceding on behalf of.

I am sure that at some point that I was gifted with the Word of Knowledge and the gift of discernment. I could feel the power of the Holy Spirit after I applied the study format prayer. In some cases, I began to state things about some of the people I could not possibly have known.

I also became aware of some negative presence in some of them and commanded it to leave. Once I had a chance to review the data, what I sensed and empirically believed happened, was confirmed by some of the responses the participants gave to the question, "What did you experience?" One female that I prayed for seemed to be under some degree of stress, so I perceived that she may have been uncomfortable with the observation process. Some of the observers made comments regarding Observation Three – Female, but she was not interviewed. I requested that a female intercessor complete the intercession. Some of the individuals I prayed for experienced the phenomenon of "Slain in or Falling under the Spirit." I did notice that the other intercessors were getting the same reaction, the catchers were very busy.

The entire prayer session took about two hours to accommodate everyone who wanted to be prayed for. I prayed/interceded for ten people – five males and five females. I personally felt that God used me to deliver some of the individuals from demons.

I collected the Deliverance Prayer Survey Observation Tool forms and the Participants Interview Responses from the four observers (two males and two females) and thanked them for their participation in the process.

Chapter Five
Post Ministry Research Event Data Review

Data Sorting and Consolidation

There were four observations for each of the ten individuals I interceded for with the Deliverance Prayer. This totaled ten observations per each observer. The final results were forty Observation Tool sheets and nine Participant Responses - one female participant's intercession was completed by another intercessor; an interview was not conducted for that participant.

The Observation Tool sheets were reviewed and compared to insure that all four observers' observation orders and genders matched. The data was verified to be uncorrupted and useable. Once that was determined, the handwritten data was typed as it appeared onto blank Observation Tool sheets for review, consolidation and sorting.

In Appendix B, the reproduced Observation Tool sheets results can be reviewed. The form has been reduced from full page to half page size so that two Observation Tool sheets can be placed on one page. The typed data sheets were checked ten times against the primary original data sheets by two sorters for an accurate transfer and to avoid corruption of the primary original data. The comments from each observation were Eye Activity, Coughing/Choking, Vomiting, Throwing Up Phlegm, Falling to the Floor, Noises, Other Body Movements and Other Observations. Noises, Other Body Movements and Other Observations allowed for narrative statements, Eye Activity through Falling on Floor were check (√) marks or (**X**) annotations. The data was also consolidated into the "Observation Tool Consolidation Chart," Appendix D. This reduced forty pages (forty observations) down to four pages of data without eliminating any data. The categories of Vomiting and Throwing up Phlegm were removed from the consolidation chart, because these areas did not have any data recorded in the ten observations from the four observers relative to the forty Observations Tool sheets.

The Observation Tool Consolidation Chart is an exact extrapolation of the information in Appendix B. For example, if you want to compare Observation 2 – Male relative to Falling on the Floor; you could review the Observation Tool sheets for Observation 2 - Male for each observer and track every entry that appears on the Observation Tool Consolidation Chart.

The Observation Tool Consolidation Chart uses a key system: F= Freddie, E = Edna, ES = Elder Steve, D = Denise, O = Observation Number, OBM = Other Body Movement, and OO = Other Observations. Each activity that was annotated on the raw data Observation Tool sheets and transferred to Appendix B, has been accounted for on the Observation Tool Consolidation Chart, using the key codes and category headings. The responses to the participant question can be reviewed in Appendix C.

For each category where an activity was recorded the key words appear. The observer and the observation appear according to the observation number and gender. The data review confirmed the integrity of data and the process, which will allow the process to continue with the evaluation and analysis.

Evaluation and Analysis

Evaluation and data analysis will focus on the data from the perspective of the type of reaction(s) and behavior(s) recorded, and the amount of occurrences observed. As a point of review, four observers observed ten participants; each participant had four different observations. Five females and five males were observed by two females and two males.

Some of the information from the Observation Tool Consolidation Chart has been extrapolated to form the Impact Reaction(s)/Behavior(s) Occurrence Table 1.

Impact Reaction(s)/Behavior(s) Occurrence Table 1

Reaction/Behaviors	Occurrences	Total of Observations
Eye Activity	10	22
Coughing/Choking	2	4
Falling	7	23
Noises	7	15
Shaking/Swaying	7	14
Crying	2	7
Fists balled	3	5
Heavy Breathing/Panting	2	4
Total	40	94

This information was extrapolated based on occurrences and total observation. This means that all four observers for Observation Six-Male recorded eye activity, would count as one occurrence not four different occurrences; but it would count as four observations. The maximum prayed for under this study was ten, the occurrences are based on the one occurrence, per participant observed. The maximum of any occurrence cannot exceed ten. Because there were four observers for each participant the maximum amount of observations could be forty, or ten times four. The occurrences represent the fact that at least one observer annotated the behavior(s) that appear on the Impact Reaction(s)/Behavior(s) Occurrence Table. The reaction(s) and behavior(s) occurrences as well as the total observations for each selected impact, in the form of reaction(s) and behavior(s), appear in Table 1.

I would like to restate the question and the informal hypothesis at this point: **Question:** "Will a specific format of Deliverance Prayer impact the lives of people in need of deliverance?

Informal Hypothesis One: There will be some recognizable impact in the form of reaction(s) and behavior(s) to a specific format of

Deliverance Prayer. The point I want to make at this juncture is that the data demonstrates that recognizable impact did occur during the specific Deliverance Prayer process. The Observation Tool Consolidation Chart and the Impact Reaction(s)/Behavior(s) Occurrence Table, reflect what the observers recorded. The Participant Impact Question Response form records what the participants experienced.

Participant Question Impact Response Review

Each response will be reviewed relative to impact in the form of reaction(s) and behavior(s).

Question: What did you experience?

Participant #1 Male Response:

> "I felt free like a bird." "It's like I could forget my past." "Light headed." "Good." "Can't express…It's the peace…I've been searching for."

This participant seemed to experience an encounter with the Holy Spirit. According to the Observation Tool Consolidation Chart this participant experienced the phenomenon called "Slain in the Spirit."

Participant #2 Male Response:

> "Like a backward pull." "As he was calling out, it was pulling from within." "I've had problems with my bowels, but I felt the peace of God there." "I have gone to many Deliverances, but always left with some feeling of freedom, but tonight I felt total freedom." "I always felt there is a point that the demons would come out, but Dr. Maddox knew that they were there and made them come out." "Praise God!"

This participant implied that a healing of the bowels may have occurred. Also, that demons had been forced to leave him. The gifts of healing and discerning of spirits appear to have been activated through the intercession. This participant experienced the phenomenon called "Slain in the Spirit."

Participant #3 Female Response:

> No interview notes, someone else   finished praying for this person

There are some observations regarding this participant in Appendix B and Appendix D. These observations seem to imply peace and a receptive spirit. My perception and what I discerned is that she was not comfortable with me, or the process of the study. The main concern was and should always be for the one who is being interceded for. I requested that one of the female intercessors complete the Deliverance Prayer process with her.

Participant #4 Female Response:

> "I was very uncomfortable, probably because I'm pregnant, [due 12/16]." "I felt the anointing, peace." " A clearer conscious." "All worries just feels gone." "He's a good teacher." "Very powerful and anointed." [She had a big smile through the interview.]

This participant implies an encounter with the anointing, peace, and clearer conscious. She believed the intercession to be anointed and powerful. The implication is that the Holy Spirit manifested during this intercession.

Participant #5 Female Response:

> "I've been prayed for before but when Dr. Maddox prayed, I really sensed in my spirit that God was involved." "It's a difference." "A very high anointing." "A lot of things he said related back to my past that he couldn't know about or what I had been through."

This participant implies that the intercessor was anointed and detected the presence of the Spirit of God. According to the participant the gift of the Holy Spirit called the Word of Knowledge was activated. This participant also experienced the phenomenon "Slain in the Spirit."

Participant #6 Male Response:

> "Felt good." "… Like something is going to happen." "Dr.
> Maddox spoke to my situation without knowing what it was but I
> knew what he was talking about." "Felt like God was doing
> something in me while I was laying down."

This participant experienced the gift of the Word of Knowledge as it was activated through the intercession that spoke to his situation. This participant experienced the phenomenon called "Slain in or Falling under the Spirit." The participant indicated that he felt that God was in him while he was "Slain in the Spirit."

Participant #7 Male Response:

> "A real calm and peace." "The things that he spoke, he spoke
> quietly, like it was a private conversation, but I heard it amplified."
> "When I was on the floor, the Lord was showing things from the
> past to me real clear. I knew he was not going to let me go back."

This participant experienced the phenomenon called "Slain in the Spirit," the instant I put my hands on his chest to pray for him. The participant felt overwhelmed by the Spirit and having his thoughts wiped out. He was aware of past events, could be "Word of Knowledge". His perception was that "God was doing His thing."

Participant #8 Male Response:

> "He didn't even begin praying." "I don't know what happened
> and all of a sudden I was encompassed by the spirit and was slayed
> under. I guess God was doing his thing." "Felt like an invasion,"
> "Overpowered." "My thoughts were wiped out, I was going to
> ask for prayers for my new position at church. I wanted to ask for
> success and to live up to the responsibility…but everything
> happened so fast."

This participant experienced the phenomenon called "Slain in the Spirit," the instant I put my hands on his chest to pray for him. The participant felt overwhelmed by the Spirit and having his thoughts wiped out. He was aware of past events, could be "Word of Knowledge". His perception was that "God was doing His thing."

Participant #9 Female Response:

> "Very refreshed and encouraged." "Felt the presence of God, like an assurance, then empowered." "Warm sensation." "Safe/secure." "Knowing that truth is being applied into your spirit…you can sense it like something was standing next to you and got inside of you, which was Jesus Christ." "Felt the warm power of God coming out of him [Dr. Maddox] into me. I wanted to stay there at that warm place."

This participant had a strong sense of the presence of God. The participant also made reference to Jesus Christ standing next to her and moving into her. She perceived that warm power of God coming out of the intercessor and into her. This participant was "Slain in the Spirit." I would recommend reading the comments made by the observers in the OBM and OO sections of the Observation Tool Consolidation Chart. A great deal of activity is annotated, such as crawling on the floor, crying, squatting, etc.

Participant #10 Female Response:

> "At one point I felt a lot of pain in my feet first time that has happened to me." "I was between the feeling of peace and pain in my feet." "I could hear and understand everything he said." "Felt real tired and peaceful." "Feet hurt a little, still; probably from standing so long."

This participant experienced some mixed emotions relative to peace, and pain in her feet. I, as intercessor, sensed that she needed deliverance from something she was not ready to address. I could see and sense her pain. I ended the intercession with an "Amen."

I would recommend a review of the Observation Tool Consolidation Chart for a deeper insight into the impact in the form of reaction(s) and behavior(s) of the participants. It is apparent that the input from the participants provided a deeper insight to the internal impact, as well as supernatural activity; Word of Knowledge, healing, casting out demons, and "Slain in or Falling under the Spirit." Table 2 has been created to consolidate the participants' impact perceptions, titled the Participant Impact Response Table 2.

Participants Impact Response Table 2

Reactions/Behavior	Occurrences
Anointing	2
Demonic Deliverance	1
Peace	3
Power	3
Presence of God	5
Slain in the Spirit	7
Word of Knowledge	3
Total	24

The Participants Impact Response Table (Table 2) is an extrapolation of the reaction(s) and behavior(s) from the Participant Question Response Form.

Again, I should at this point restate the question and the informal hypothesis.

Question: Will a specific form of Deliverance Prayer impact the lives of people in need of deliverance?

Informal Hypothesis One: There will be some recognizable impact in the form of reaction(s) and behavior(s) to a specific format of Deliverance Prayer.

Chapter Six
Post Ministry Event-Impact Evaluation Interviews

As it has been stated earlier in this study, ten individuals were prayed for without any provision for follow-up. Follow up was not part of the original design. However, when I discovered that four out of the ten could be contacted via the Session Leader I developed a four question "Post Ministry Event - Impact Interview Form" (see page 100) and contacted the participants for an interview. The addition of the post interview has broadened the scope of the Ministry Event beyond the immediate impact analysis date of November 8, 2002. Three females and one male were identified and contacted, they agreed to respond to the four interview questions. The same method that was used to identify them in the study, see Appendices B, C, and D, will be used relative to the "Post Ministry Event - Impact Interview Form," see Appendix E. The respondents were Female Observation Four, Male Observation Eight, Female Observation Nine, and Female Observation Ten. These interviews were conducted by telephone. I will present the questions and the responses to each question in groupings for simplification of the response review process.

Receiving feedback from participants from over a four-month period after the Ministry Research Event, did provide additional impact feedback data. This added component enhanced the outcome of the treatise/study relative to a time lapsed ministry event impact.

Post Ministry Event-Impact Interview Form

Gender of Participate:_____
Observation:_____

Post Ministry Event – Impact Interview Questions and Responses

1. Why did you come forth for deliverance prayer?

Response:

2. Had you had deliverance prayer before?

Response:

3. What has happened in the way of on going deliverance as a result of the November 8, 2002, prayer?

Response

4. Did this particular deliverance prayer make a difference?

Response:

Post Ministry Event-Impact Evaluation Interview Questions and Responses Summary

1. Why did you come forth for deliverance prayer?

Female Observation Four Response: "I do not remember."

Male Observation Eight Response: "Dealing with issues, mostly lusts of the eyes and flesh."

Female Observation Nine Response: "I needed deliverance from grief-heaviness as a result of my son's death.

Female Observation Ten Response: "I had a great deal of anger."

2. Had you had deliverance prayer before?

Female Observation Four Response: "Yes."

Male Observation Eight Response: "Yes."

Female Observation Nine Response: "Yes."

Female Observation Ten Response: "Yes."

3. What has happened in the way of on going deliverance as a result of the November 8, 2002 prayer?

Female Observation Four Response: "What was said came to pass, depression was lifted."

Male Observation Eight Response: "I look at women differently with more respect."

Female Observation Nine Response: "Freedom from over burden of grief- heaviness."

Female Observation Ten Response: "I was delivered from demonic anger, and now can recognize it and bind it when it rises. I can ask myself why the anger is there. I could not do this before."

4.   Did this particular deliverance prayer make a difference?

Female Observation Four Response: "Felt the same as other deliverance prayers. God is the one doing the work."

Male Observation Eight Response: "Yes, it did."

Female Observation Nine Response: "Yes, I felt empowered and delivered!"

Female Observation Ten Response: "Yes, I got in touch with the Spirit. I can recognize demonic anger when it comes up."

Analysis

Three of the respondents remembered why they came forth for prayer. Female Observation Four did not remember. The responses revealed that all of the respondents had been involved in deliverance prayer prior to the, November 8, 2002, ministry event. All of the respondents acknowledged that they have experienced something in the way of an ongoing deliverance as a result of the November 8, 2002, prayer. All but one respondent, Female Observation Four believed that the prayer prayed on November 8, 2002 made a difference. Through this process I was able to gather information relative to impact in the form of reaction(s) and behavior(s) for over a four-month period, November 8, 2002, through March 25, 2003. The documented feedback was derived from forty percent of the study's original participant population of ten. This is significant relative to event impact over a period of time as it relates to a specific format of deliverance prayer. It is understood that other variables, over the four-month period could have come into play. Given the fact that the respondents have been prayed for before, they are in the best position to articulate and compare the affects short and long range of the November 8, 2002, prayer to other deliverance prayers they have been exposed to. The Post Ministry Event Impact Evaluation Interview process did establish that impact in the form of reaction(s) and behavior(s) did extended beyond the initial ministry event. How this data is interpreted in the deliverance ministry/spiritual warfare arena is another question for another study. The established fact is that the data did respond to the study/treatise Question and Informal Hypothesis One in the affirmative. It has been confirmed and recorded as evidence that impact occurred on November 8, 2002. The net learning from the Post Ministry Event-Impact Evaluation Interview responses is that in studies of this nature, a mechanism to evaluate impact beyond the initial ministry event impact is imperative. The process now must take form relative to how I and others will reflect on the impact of this event, in relationship to inner healing and deliverance ministry/spiritual warfare activity.

Chapter Seven
Reflection

Major Accomplishments of This Treatise/Study

Research

The Theory/Literature Review chapter addressed the major and some of the minor controversies in the inner healing and deliverance ministry/spiritual warfare arena. Before the question of this treatise/study could be broached, some of the controversies had to be explored. This served not only to set the question on a foundation in order to proceed, but provided information from different perspectives.

Ministry event

The fact that this process was allowed to occur within an established inner healing and deliverance ministry/spiritual warfare environment, was an accomplishment in itself. Most of this arena, if not all, is closed to investigative research, because of the tension that exists between practitioners and theorists. The inner healing and deliverance ministry/spiritual warfare environments are very skeptical about allowing academia to do any research in their environments. Fear is the major reason for the lack of trust; they have apprehension regarding the persons conducting the research. They fear a product that is uncomplimentary to their environment in particular, and the arena as a whole. This fear is partially based on the concern that most academic researchers do not have a practical background in the inner healing and deliverance ministry/spiritual warfare arena. A review of the deliverance history section reveals some of the reasons for this lack of trust.

I had to develop a relationship for over fifteen months to be allowed to conduct this study in an inner healing and deliverance spiritual warfare ministry environment, that is internationally known. The main reasons this was possible is because I have over thirty years' experience with supernatural encounters, and my background as an inner healing and deliverance ministry/spiritual warfare practitioner aided in building the trust factor.

The Learning

Academically I have been exposed to more resource material during this period than any period in my journey. There has been an explosion of learning relative to the inner healing and deliverance ministry/spiritual warfare arena, augmenting what I knew empirically. From my perspective, I know that Deliverance Prayer will and has had an impact on those seeking deliverance.

Study Limitations and Challenges

As stated previously, the deliverance ministry/spiritual warfare arena is very particular as to whom they allow to observe their activities under any circumstances, especially for research purposes. The fact that this study took place in an established deliverance/ spiritual warfare environment was an accomplishment of its own. It must be pointed out, considering the Treatise/Study question, that the only validating venue for the event had to be a recognized established inner healing and deliverance ministry/spiritual warfare location. Objectivity is always a challenge and it is not realistic to believe that it can be authentically produced in any situation. In this study the goal was to strive for objectivity. The fact is that no one is objective, they can only attempt to be. The environment where the study took place was pro deliverance, and all of the observers were pro deliverance/spiritual warfare practitioners. Participants were aware in advance, and the ones who were not aware, because they were attending these services for the first time, still had some prior knowledge and preconceived notion of what to expect. In order to get permission participants had to be informed before the event. Having made those statements, I realize that my inclination would have been to view the impact in the form of reaction(s) and behavior(s) through the lens of a pro deliverance spiritual warfare practitioner. The impact outcomes were presented from a mixed perspective of qualitative, quantitative and interpretative analysis with neither being a pure scientific form relative to this process. Although, scientific and academic elements were presented throughout this process, they were impacted by the elusive nature of the supernatural. There was a tradeoff between the location (environment) of the study, and what some may call pure objectivity. I am confident that the tradeoff is what allowed this unprecedented study to take place, therefore paving the way for other studies relative to Deliverance Prayer and Deliverance Ministry.

This study was by design intended to be an introduction to a part of what happens in the inner healing deliverance ministry/spiritual warfare arena, specifically Deliverance Prayer. Ministry event participant impact feedback was initially limited to reaction(s) and behavior(s) that were observed and to what the participants were able to articulate to the interviewer, the evening of the event. The process was not intended to compare other prayer outcomes and styles or to do any time lapsed individual impact follow-up. An attempt was made through the Session Leader to make contact with the individuals prayed for. This was done in order to broaden the scope of the Ministry Event. Four out of the ten were located and contacted by me. A four-question interview with the four respondents was conducted, see Chapter Six and Appendix E for results.

The post impact interview process did reveal that participants continued to experience some impact, in excess of one hundred thirty seven days beyond the initial ministry event. Some peripheral issues were broached out of necessity; some received more attention than others. An attempt was made to provide some research that opposed my practitioner's mindset from a cross section of authors, with varied backgrounds. These limitations are acknowledged and could be subjects for future studies in the area of Deliverance Prayer. Some of the literature was reviewed after the Ministry Research Event took place, resulting in some enhanced insights relative to the process, see chapter two.

All research studies contain margin of errors or variables that influence or impact outcomes. In regards to this study, several areas of challenge or impacting variables should be stated:

- Personality of the Intercessor

- Experience of the Intercessor

- Experience of the Observers

☐ The Nature of the Reactions

☐ Perceptions of the Observers

☐ Perceptions of the Interviewers

☐ Alertness of the Observers

☐ Participants Playing Into the Process

☐ Counterfeit Spirit Influence

☐ Access to the Deliverance Arena

Except for one or two, all of the stated challenges would be true for any research study. The data speaks for itself. All of the limitations, challenges and restrictions of this study were not design generated. Some limitations of this study are/were a result of the elusive nature of the supernatural. Other limitations are/were based on the perceptions of individuals, institutions, and theological articulations, they are beyond the control and scope of this study. As stated in the introduction; studies that probe into the religious supernaturalism or areas where man may not control may cause a negative response to the one who is doing the probing. I am reminded of Wilson Brian Key's statement in *Subliminal Seduction*:

> This view of man as being dominated by a mechanism within his mind of which he has no conscious knowledge is to many a frightening attack upon the ego. Anyone who incautiously probes into unconscious perceptions or motives may wind up ridiculed by an outraged, self-righteous mob. (Key, 1973, p. 47)

I also acknowledge that my pro deliverance practitioner mindset may conflict with the liturgy of others.

There may be debate regarding what the impact in the form of reaction(s) and behavior(s) mean, but no debate relative to impact manifestations. There may be debate about whether or not the specific format of prayer that was prayed generated the impact. Follow-up researchers are invited to examine and prove that the prayer used did not generate the impact occurrences documented in this study.

The fact remains that this study did fulfill its goals; impact in the form of reaction(s) and behavior(s) did manifest as a result of a specific format of Deliverance Prayer. The debate may occur in relationship to the limitations, interpretation and meaning relative to ministry, but not the impact relative to the question. The study's focus was to determine if impact would occur, and the study accomplished that mission. This study will provide a springboard for other studies in this arena, because it will serve as a land mine locator map. I stand firmly behind the process and the findings of this study.

Chapter Eight
Study Process Impact

Overview

This treatise/study has demonstrated impact in the form of reaction(s) and behavior(s) on the study participants/subject. Relative to the ten participants that were prayed for impact was documented on November 8, 2002, and again for forty percent of the participants, on March 25, 2003. The fact that the respondents on March 25, 2003 articulated some degree of continued impact over a one hundred thirty five day period, is significant relative to time lapsed impact.

There were other study participants who were not direct targets of the study such as: the Observation Team, the Session Leader, Dissertation Committee, my immediate family, and myself.

I will focus on process impact relative to myself at this point in my journey. I will use a reflective question approach to accomplish impact analysis. However, I do intend to spend some time writing about the process impact relative to the other indirect study participants sometime in the future.

Project Impact

I would have to say that the process has reinforced expectations of my reality relative to what can happen when you approach something outside of the acceptable status quo; namely resistance. I found it very difficult to secure a study location because of factors that were previously stated. Working in an environment that is the leadership responsibility of someone else required a level of submission I had not achieved/attained before. I have learned some valuable lessons that have strengthened me as a leader.

In the religious and academic arenas I continued to face ongoing resistance, covert subtle as well as overt resistance, to the concept that inner healing and deliverance ministry/spiritual warfare are legitimate ministry activities. This was true of the entire experience, not just the project process. The process in fact for me was and is spiritual warfare. To clarify my perspective, evil supernaturalism, in the form of Satan, demons, evil spirits, principalities and powers in the context in which they have been described in the Theory/Literature Review chapter were/are poised to prevent the completion of this process. I believe in supernatural confrontation and I also believe that this dissertation process has stirred up a conflict in the evil supernatural realm.

> What is most crucial about this situation, biblically speaking, is the failure of moral theology, in the American context, to confront the principalities, institutions, systems, ideologies, and other political and social powers- as militant, aggressive, and immensely influential creatures in this world as it is. (Wylie-Kellerman, 1991, p. 71)

> Every Power tends to have a visible pole, and outer form- be it a church, a nation, or an economy- and an invisible pole, an inner spirit or driving force that animates, legitimates, and regulates its physical manifestation in the world. (Wink, 1984, p.5)

The point that I am making in conjunction with Wylie-Kellerman and Wink is that the supernatural has impact relative to all structures engaged by humans. I am in the business of exposing the evil supernatural therefore I am their enemy. Being an enemy of the evil supernatural elements means you come under attack by everything or mechanism, controlled or influenced by that realm. I recognize of course that many do not believe or accept the concept of evil supernatural control or influence over people or structures. As a spiritual warrior, I must speak from my knowledge, experience and academic training. This process has made me more intense in addressing what I believe, relative to the truth. There is always a risk in stating what you believe, I accept that risk.

Questions Raised

I will list some of the questions raised by this treatise/study and respond to them. Other questions raised by this process have been addressed in previous sections of this study.

Question: Why not do a comparative prayer study with at least two prayers instead of the one specific format?

Response: It was difficult securing a location for reasons stated under Ministry Event, in chapter seven. Attempting to do a multifaceted Ministry Event under those conditions would not have been advisable or allowed. Another complication would have necessitated putting together another team of observers, and conducting a parallel prayer event or set up another event using the same observers. The comparative prayer scenario seems great if you have the staff, your own environment, and the time required to do the background research for this type of study. Neither were available to me at the time of this study. Nevertheless, the most important rationale was, it was not the focus for this study.

Question: Why not a long range study?

Response: A long range project from my perspective would be over a two year period. This type of study would take time to establish relationships that would allow for multiple study locations, and to recruit and train observation teams. To attempt a long range or a multiple event study, at the point this study was conducted, would have drawn more criticism. The one ministry event, with immediate impact observation was the methodology I could promote to the Session Leader at that point in our relationship.

Question: Why study something you cannot see or measure?

Response: The Journey chapter of this treatise/study covers the rationale or motivation for this treatise/study. Inner healing and deliverance ministry/spiritual warfare has been my focus for over three decades, I was driven to do this study. The degree of measurability of course is outside natural standards of measurability because of the supernatural structure of the subject.   The fact is Christianity, is a supernatural concept with elements such as: resurrection, going to Heaven or Hell, and God the Father, Son and Holy Spirit.   Millions pursue Christianity every day, and it is measurable based on impact in the form of reaction(s) and behavior(s) manifested in the lives of those who call themselves Christians.   This process was a beginning relative to gauging the impact of a specific format of Deliverance Prayer.   As research in this area continues, theories and methodologies will be developed to improve the measurability of the supernatural inducing phenomenon called Deliverance Prayer.

Question: How would you conduct a future study?

Response: I   would   conduct   the   study   in   three   different locations/environments, under three different denominational banners. One would be an inner healing and deliverance ministry/spiritual warfare banner; the other two would be from other so-called major denominations.   I would attempt to engage an African-American, European, and Hispanic cultural environments.   Three different Deliverance Prayer formats would be employed at each study location. The ministry event would occur for one year, with six months of prayer and six months of follow-up impact evaluation. There would be a separate observation team for each location.   The Methodology would basically be the same as this study, except where the proposed new model would necessitate modification.   This is the recommended model for a future study. The reasons why this study was not conducted in this new model recommendations have been articulated and identified in some detail in this treatise/study.   One of the most important reasons is the experience and learning that took place during this process, was not available prior to this process.

The impact and learning relative to this process is ongoing.   The benefit and value I believe is also ongoing.

Present Journey

I am currently pastoring and have been for almost seven years. I have been in ministry for over twenty-five years, and I am elated to be in open warfare as a Pastor against the hordes of hell. My journey relative to the Doctor of Ministry at the Ecumenical Theological Seminary, in Detroit, has been a factor in equipping me to advance the ministries of inner healing, and deliverance and to become a more educated, articulate and skilled proponent of spiritual warfare.

Relative to this treatise/study, a foundation has been laid for some understanding relative to this arena from a perspective that many will be able to relate to. I have stated, several times throughout the assembling of this study, I had one main focus, that one main focus was and is "To ascertain and document the impact of a specific format of Deliverance Prayer". This focus necessitated in depth research to address the level of rejection, fear, ignorance, disbelief, flawed theology, religion, doctrine and denial surrounding the topics of demons and the impact they have on the Christian Church.

What I have discovered is that the information is available, from writers of every denominational background and theology, relative to understanding deliverance and evil supernaturalism. Of course, there are some writers who would advocate that the whole issue of spiritual warfare, and Christians having a need to understand the process is a foolish waste of time. What I have discovered is the exact opposite.

One of my concerns in the arena of deliverance ministry and spiritual warfare is the disconnect between the scholarly body of knowledge and the deliverance practitioner who operates in the power of what is called "the anointing." Some in deliverance ministry/spiritual warfare feel that God will show them directly what they need to know and do, without any reading, without formal or informal learning or training experiences. Others believe the only way to do deliverance ministry is from a formal textbook diagram lead approach; intellectual versus empirical. The reality is that a balance has to be achieved and maintained. Note: 2 Peter 1: 5 - 8, and I Corinthians 8:1.

> And beside this, giving all diligence, add to your faith virtue; and to virtue knowledge; And to knowledge temperance; and to temperance patience; and to patience godliness; And to godliness brotherly kindness; and to brotherly kindness charity. For if these things be in you, and abound, they make

you that ye shall neither be barren nor unfruitful in the knowledge of our Lord Jesus Christ. (2 Peter 1:5-8, KJV)

"Now as touching things offered unto idols, we know that we all have knowledge. Knowledge puffeth up, but charity edifieth" (1 Corinthians 8:1 KJV).

There is an important balance between things that are derived from study, academia and things derived from the Spirit, divine revelation. Sometimes the lines are blurred, however, in most cases very distinguishable. I intend to demonstrate that balance, in my practice of deliverance ministry/spiritual warfare.

The data suggests that supernatural events occurred during this study: Healing, Word of Knowledge, Slain or Falling in or Under the Spirit, Casting out Demons, and the presence of Jesus Christ entering someone. The data also revealed that events normally associated with demon deliverance, like vomiting and throwing up phlegm did not occur. I would like to submit that the command Deliverance Prayer used in the study was from Dr. Mitchell who had prayed that God would stop demonic demonstrations in his deliverance ministry including vomiting, etc.

In 1973, the morning after a particularly 'active' deliverance session, I prayed like this; 'Dear Lord Jesus. I know that when you came down from the Mount of Transfiguration, a demon threw the boy, whom your disciples had been trying to heal, to the ground in a convulsion (Mark 9:20). If that happened in front of you, if may be that I have to see these demonstrations, too. But, if it is all right with you, I would love them to stop.' I have rarely seen another demonic demonstration from that day to this! Is it true in this ministry that we often do not have, because we do not ask. (Mitchell, 1999, p.159)

Maybe the use of the prayer from a book of a man who has requested in prayer that convulsive demonstrations cease was honored when I used the prayer in this study.

The outcome could be considered an impact occurrence or a reaction connected to this study prayer; debatable but not disprovable. For the last fifteen months, with the exception of three or four Fridays, I have been involved in spiritual warfare deliverance sessions at which I did not use Mitchell's prayer form. At every session, there were individuals vomiting or throwing up phlegm; this did not happen relative to any of the ten people I prayed for on November 8, 2002, when I used the prayer from Dr. Mitchell's book; the impact is clear to me.

Future Journey - Conclusion

I will continue to stand as an inner healing and deliverance ministry/spiritual warfare advocate. I will utilize my God directed empirical experience combined with education and research. I also intend to complete other research projects relative to the impact of prayer on the demonic realm.

I believe the data from this study answered the question of the treatise/study in the affirmative. The informal hypothesis was not rejected by the data. And the goals set forth have been realized. I would like to restate the question, informal hypothesis one and goals at this point:
Question: Will a specific format of deliverance prayer impact the lives of people in need of deliverance?

Informal Hypothesis/Theory One: There will be some recognizable impact in the form of reaction(s) and behavior(s) to a specific format of Deliverance Prayer.

Goals: The goals are to ascertain whether or not impact in the form of reaction(s) and behavior(s) will occur as a result of a specific Deliverance Prayer, and annotate the types and nature of the reaction(s) and behavior(s) of the individuals prayed for:

1. Categorize each impact based on the type of reaction(s) and behavior(s) that manifest during the prayer.
2. Respond to the question using the data collected during the study process.

Many conversations with deliverance colleagues connected to the purpose of this study have taken place. Some feel I will come under attack for attempting this study, by both those individuals who support and do not support Deliverance Ministry. It was suggested by friends to keep it simple in something in the area of research that will make people feel "warm and fuzzy." I was warned that this "can of worms" could jeopardize my graduation. I had to do what God put on my heart. In this journey I have had to address the target as well as some peripheral questions that manifested during the process. Peripheral distractions can contaminate or enhance the target issue. This study demanded that I spend some time with some peripheral subject matter. A caveat of this approach is that peripheral subject matter did create questions that could not fully be addressed. I do believe that credibility was a by-product of the peripheral subject matter endeavor.

I plan to continue to analyze this whole process, relative to the impact it has had on me and others in my life. I want to understand how demonic forces, principalities or powers have come against me and this process, during this phase of my journey. I must state that I believe I came under, and that I am still under attack. If the process is to produce long range and continuous ministry outcomes, those outcomes are going to have to be birthed through me, in the form of more effective service to my congregation and community. I am a veteran in the arena of supernatural conflict, and I have sensed the evidence of conflict in the demonic realm. I know and accept the fact that controversy surrounds inner healing and deliverance/spiritual warfare ministry, because of the evil supernatural influences. I will spend the immediate future evaluating, evaluating, and evaluating. I will continue to participate in deliverance meetings, possibly establish a new location. The learning process will continue, as well as the teaching process. It must be pointed out that this study from Journey to Reflection is a significant ministry event. It has and will serve the needs of many who are in environments that refuse to broach, consider, and address the realm of the demonic supernatural, and the continuous damage being inflicted by it.

My Focus

The Spirit of the Lord is upon me, because he hath anointed me to preach the gospel to the poor; he hath sent me to heal the brokenhearted, to preach deliverance to the captives, and recovering of sight to the blind, to set at liberty them that are bruised, To preach the acceptable year of the Lord. (Luke 4:18-19 KJV)

And he said unto them, Go ye into all the world, and preach the gospel to every creature. He that believeth and is baptized shall be saved; but he that believeth not shall be damned. And these signs shall follow them that believe; In my name shall they cast out devils; they shall speak with new tongues; They shall take up serpents; and if they drink any deadly thing, it shall not hurt them; they shall lay hands on the sick, and they shall recover. (Mark 16:15-18 KJV)

MINISTRY IS A SERVICE AND SERVICE IS A SACRIFICE

References

Barnes, A. (1992). *Barnes' notes*, P.C. Bible (Version 2) [Computer Softwear]. Seattle, WA: BibleSoft.

Boyd, G.A. (1997). *God at war: The Bible and spiritual conflict.* Downers Grove, IL: InterVarsity Press.

Brill, A.A. (Ed.). (1966) The basic writings of Sigmund Freud (S. Freud, Author). New York: Random House, Inc. (Original work published 1938)

Brown, R. (1997). *An introduction to the new testament.* New York: Doubleday.

Brown, R., M.D. (1992). *He came to set the captives free.* New Kensington, PA: Whitaker House.

Buttrick, G.A., Kepler, T.S., Knox, J., May, H.G., Terrien, S., & Bucke, E.S.(Eds.). (1962). *The interpreter's dictionary of the Bible.* New York: Abington Press.

Chavda, M. (1998). *Prayer and fasting.* Shippensburg, PA: Destiny Images.

Eckhardt, Apostle J. (1998). Crusaders church and international ministries of prophetic and apostolic churches.
In C. Peter Wagner (Ed.), *The new apostolic churches* (pp. 45 - 58). Ventura, CA: Regal Books.

Foster, K. N. (2001). *Sorting out the supernatural.* Camp Hill, PA: Christian Publications.

Frangipane, F. (1989). *The three battlegrounds.* Cedar Rapids, IA: Arrow Publications.

Garrison, M. (1980). *How to conduct spiritual warfare, as I see it!* Hudson, FL: Mary Garrison.

Hagin, K. E. (1981). *Why do people fall under the power?* Tulsa, OK: Faith Library Publications.

Hagin, K.E. (1991). *The Holy Spirit and His gifts*. Tulsa, OK: Faith Library Publications.

Hammond, F. & Hammond, I. M. (1973). *Pigs in the parlor.* Kirkwood, MO: Impact Christian Books, Inc.

Henry, M. (1992). *Matthew Henry's commentary*, P.C. Bible (Version 2) [Computer Softwear]. Seattle, WA: BibleSoft.

Hinn, B. (1995). *Welcome Holy Spirit.* Nashville: Thomas Nelson Publishers.

Holdcroft, L.T. (1979). The Holy Spirit, a Pentecostal interpretation. Springfield, MO: Gospel Publishing House.

Holy Bible, King, James version, (KJV). Oxford: Oxford Press.
Holy Bible, new King James version, (NKJ). Nashville: Thomas Nelson Publishers.

Ing, R. (1996). *Spiritual warfare.* New Kensington, PA: Whitaker House.

Joyner, R. (n.d.). Azusa street: The fire that could not die. Retrieved April 22, 2003, from (http://www.evanwiggs.com/revival/history/fire.html)

Key, W.B. (1973). *Subliminal Seduction: Ad media's manipulation of a not so innocent America.* Englewwod Cliffs, NJ: Prentice-Hall, Inc.

Kraft, C. H (1992). *Defeating dark angels.* Ann Arbor: Servant Publishing.

Larson, B. (1999). *Larson's book of spiritual warfare.* Nashville: Thomas Nelson Publishers.

MacNutt, F., o.p. (1977). *The power to heal.* Notre Dame, IN: Ave Maria Press.

MacNutt, F (1995). *Deliverance from evil spirits, a practical manual.* Grand Rapids: Chosen Books.

McAlpine, T. H. (1991). Facing the powers – What are the options? Monrovia, CA: MARC.

Mitchell, L. D. (1999). *Liberty in Jesus.* Durham, England: The Pentland Press.

Moody, G.B. (1998). *Deliverance manual.* Baton Rouge, LA: Deliverance Ministries

Monroe, Dr. M. (2000). Understanding the purpose and power of prayer, earthly *license for heavenly interference* New Kensington, PA: Whitaker House.

Murphy, Dr. E. (1996). *The handbook for spiritual warfare.* Nashville: Thomas Nelson Publishers.

Peck, M.D., M.S. (1983). *People of the lie.* New York: Simon and Shuster.

Prince, D. (1998). *They shall expel demons.* Grand Rapids: Chosen Books.

Raboteau, A.J. (1978). *Slave religion – The 'invisible institution in the Antebellum south.* Oxford: Oxford Press.

Rice, T.W. (2003). Believe it or not: Religious and other paranormal beliefs in the United States. *Journal for the Scientific Study of Religion, 42,* p. 96 – 106.

Robeson, Dr. J. & Robeson, Dr. C. (1997). *Stongman's his name...II, Biblical answers to spiritual warfare questions.* Woodburn, OR: Shiloh Publishing House.

Ryrie, Charles C. (1997). *The Holy Spirit.* Chicago; Moody Press. Sanford, J.L. and Sanford, M. (1992). *A comprehensive guide to deliverance and inner healing.* Grand Rapids: Chosen Books.

Sherrer, Q. & Garlock, R. (1992). *The spiritual warrior's prayer guide.* Ann Arbor, MI: Servant Publication.

Slavin, R.E. (1992). *Research methods in education,* second edition. Boston: Allyn and Bacon.

Vincent, M.R. (1992). *Vincent's NT Word Studies.* P.C. Bible (Version 2) [Computer Softwear]. Seattle, WA: BibleSoft.

Weber, S. (2001). *Spirit warriors.* Sisters, OR: Mulmomah Publishers.

Whyte, H. A. M. (1973). *Casting out demons.* New Kensington, PA: Whitaker House.

Whyte, H. A. M. (1989). *Demons & deliverance.* New Kensington, PA: Whitaker House.

Wink, W. (1984). *Naming the powers.* Philadelphia: Fortress Press.

Wink, W. (1986). *Unmasking the powers.* Philadelphia: Fortress Press.

Wink, W. (1992). *Engaging the powers: discernment and resistance in a world of domination.* Mineapolis: Fortress Press.

Worley, W. (1976). *Battling the hosts of hell– diary of an exoricist.* Lansing, IL: W.R.W.

Wylie-Kellermann, B. (1991). Season of faith and conscience: Kairos, confessilitrugy. Maryknoll, NY: Orbis.

Wylie-Kellerman, B. (1998, March/April). Exorcising an American demon: Racism as a principality, *Soujourner*, 9 – 12.

Zuendel, F. (2000). *The awakening.* Farmington, PA: The Plough Publishing House.

Appendix A
Selected References Reviews

Brown, Rebecca, M.D., (1992). *He Came to Set the Captives Free* [book].

This author walks you through personal experience with the occult, witches, warlocks, demons, and Satan. The author records spiritual warfare and deliverance in a way few have done to date. The author suggests that the spirit world is connected to the physical world, and every action in the physical world reverberates through the spirit world.

> Most Christians are quite unaware not only of the spirit world, but of the fact that every action we take in our physical world also affects the spirit world. Charles G. Finney describes this cause and effect relationship between the physical and spiritual world beautifully: 'Every Christian makes an impression by his conduct, and witnesses either for one side or the other. His looks, dress, whole demeanor, make a constant impression on one side or the other. He cannot help testifying for or against religion. He is either gathering with Christ, or scattering abroad. At every step you tread on chords that will vibrate to all eternity. Every time you move, you touch keys whose sound will reecho all over the hills and dales of heaven, and through all the dark caverns and vaults of hell. Every movement of your lives, you are exerting a tremendous influence that will tell on the immortal interests of souls all around you.' The Last Call... For Revival, by J.T.C., p. 31. (sic) (Brown, 1992, p. 101)

This book reveals a level of demonic activity that is controversial but documentable. The significance of Dr. Brown's contribution, in my opinion, has to be in the revelation of the level of activity in the demonic realm, and the effects on human beings

Chavda, Mahesh (1998). *Prayer and Fasting* [book].

This book focuses on prayer and fasting as the main weapons of warfare against demonic strongholds. The author's background with the "mentally handicapped" was his introduction to the realm of the demonic confrontation, and he feels prayer and fasting destroys the works of the enemy.

> The key to defeating dark strongholds is twofold. First we must tap the *power* of the Spirit through the combination of prayer and fasting; and second, we will overcome in the largest battles in this generation only when we pray and fast *together* and unlash the incredible power of the Body of Christ on its knees. The Lord has commissioned me to help train up an army of men and women who will do the works of Jesus. An unavoidable part of the *works* of Jesus begins with *prayer and fasting* because these were the *first works of Jesus* in His mission to destroy the works of the enemy. (Chavda, 1998, p.74)

This author's most significant contribution could be the demonstration of the power of prayer and fasting in spiritual deliverance.

Eckhardt, Apostle John (1998). Crusaders Church and International Ministries of Prophetic and Apostolic Churches. In C. Peter Wagner (Ed.), *The New Apostolic Churches* (pp. 45 – 58) [book excerpt].

This book addresses the face of the New Apostolic Church age in the many congregational manifestations. In chapter three, Eckhardt identifies the importance of confronting the powers and principalities using the power released through the apostolic impartation from God.

> The first thing the Lord gave the Twelve when He sent them out was 'power against unclean spirits' (Matt. 10: 1 (KJV) . The apostolic anointing is therefore recognized in the spirit realm. A level of power – an authority that is released through apostles and apostolic churches – must be acknowledged by the demonic and angelic realm. This is

important if we are to be successful. What happens in the natural realm is governed by the spirit realm. ...

... This understanding is especially necessary for significant breakthroughs in the inner cities of America, as well as in the nations of the 10/40 Window. The principalities and powers that have gripped multitudes of people for so long must be challenged by implementing this kind of power and authority. (Eckhardt, 1998, p. 50)

This contribution to the field is significant relative to the apostolic movement and the spiritual warfare focus that should be a part of that movement.

Foster, K. Neill (2001). *Sorting Out the Supernatural* [book].

A scholarly work that takes aim at some of what is known as common behavior in some spiritual warfare deliverance arenas.

IN THIS CHAPTER WE ARE TALKING about what is commonly called "falling under the power." I must confess that I am not a happy writer. I don't want to write about true and false in this area since even the idea of "true" falling offends my sense of propriety and probably my pride (which God has determined to resist ahead of time – I Peter 5:5). However, to follow the inner mandate and to handle this book with integrity, falling as a religious and spiritual phenomenon, like many other things, must be divided into true and false. Indeed, so influential a figure as John Wimber said this, 'There's no place in the Bible where people were lined up and Jesus or Paul or anyone else went along and bopped them on the head and watched them go down, and somebody else ran along behind. Can you picture Peter and James—'Hold it, hold it, hold it!' —running behind trying to catch them? And so the model we're seeing, either on stage or on television, is totally different from anything that's in scripture.' (Foster, 2001, p.287)

What I respect is that Foster is willing to be transparent about his biases. "I will use several illustrations which both reveal the polarities which we are addressing and the biases of my own heart" (Foster, 2001, p. 287). In my opinion, that statement, which I believe among all of his other significant contributions in this book, is the most significant contribution. Simply because, to display his biases uncovers/reveals one of the conflicts within the spiritual warfare culture.

Frangipane, Francis (1989). *The Three Battlegrounds* [book].

This author identifies three areas of spiritual warfare as his purpose and focus. The author contends that most of us will face conflict in these three areas.

> Thus, our purpose here is to help equip you for battle in each of the three primary battlegrounds: the mind, the church and the heavenly places. There are other fields or subcategories of spiritual warfare; however, these are where most of us will face conflict. (Frangipane, 1989, p. 7)

I find the comment on the three areas of warfare interesting, especially naming the heavenly places as a spiritual battleground. My thoughts are that the perspective of this author is a valuable contribution.

Garrison, Mary (1980). *How to Conduct Spiritual Warfare, as I See It!* [book]

This author's focus is on how spiritual warfare should be waged and against whom.

> Notice that we are the ones expected to wrestle. We are not fighting people made of flesh and blood, but against unseen persons without bodies...great evil princes...huge numbers of evil spirits. We are fighting principalities...rulers, leaders, executives, chiefs, heads, masterminds, controllers, and main strongmen.... In addition to the principal strongmen spirits listed in the book, **How to Try a Spirit**, there are the living wicked spirits who have rejected Christ and chosen Satan. These are not the possessed nor bound, therefore are not in need of deliverance. **Their human spirits** are the actual strongmen that must be bound and dealt with by the Believers.

Because **they** are high ranking principal forces in the satanic kingdom. **They** control and direct demons. These are called Witches, Mediums, Fortune Tellers, Psychics, Magicians, and Sorcerers. (Garrison, 1980, p, 38 - 39)

This author is straight forward and direct relative to identifying Satan, demons, and other wicked spirits, as the main source of the problems of mankind. This author identifies symptoms of psychic attack, and some of the altered truths that Satan uses to counterfeit the Kingdom of God. The most significant contribution this author makes from my perspective is the detail given relative to the enemy's strategies.

Hammond, Frank & Hammond, Ida Mae (1973). *Pigs in the Parlor* [sic] [book].

These authors makes some interesting statements in my opinion about warfare, prayer, and deliverance.

WARFARE IS NOT PRAYER! It is in addition to prayer! There is no point in petitioning God for something He has already given you. God has given us power and authority over the devil. We must not expect God to get the devil off our backs. He has already defeated Satan and given us the ability and responsibility to take care of ourselves. This truth is a revelation to many believers—it is good news! No wonder so many prayers have seemed unanswered. We need to stop storming heaven for what has already been provided, and start using what God had given us. (Hammond & Hammond, 1973, p.14)

The process of expelling demons is called deliverance. Deliverance is not a panacea—a cure all. Yet it is an important part of what God is doing in relationship to the current revival of the church. Some expect too much from deliverance and others expect too little. We honestly need to find out what part deliverance can play in each of our own lives and receive whatever benefit it offers. (Hammond & Hammond, 1973, p.19)

This from my perspective, sets the tone of the book and adds a dimension to the arena of spiritual deliverance that could be called personal accountability; a major contribution from where I sit.

Ing, Richard, (1996). *Spiritual Warfare* [book].

This author's focus is to restore the knowledge of deliverance to the body of Christ. He views his book as a spiritual warfare manual.

> This manual attempts to dispel unnecessary fear and to create a simple pattern which most Christians can follow... Casting out demons is not new to the church -just forgotten.   God is restoring deliverance to the body of Christ today, so we need a knowledge of deliverance and spiritual warfare. (Ing, 1996, p. 7 - 8)

I would support that one of this offering's main contributions is the detailed discussion on the demonic kingdoms, realms, and hierarchies.

Kraft, Charles H., (1992). *Defeating Dark Angels* [book].

Charles Kraft addresses the basics of demonic operations, influences and casting them out. What stood out for me was his discourse on communicating with demons and the relationship that communication with demons has to deliverance.

> Ministering to people like Linda is a tremendous blessing. Unfortunately, we encounter many others like her in our ministry, people who have had negative deliverance experiences. More often than not, their deliverances failed because the ministers did not know how to get the information they needed to get the demons out and keep them out.
>
> Getting information from demons is an invaluable tool in helping the wounded. Repeatedly, I have seen God bring his healing and love through our forcing information from demons. (Kraft, 1992, p. 165)

This insight (demonic interrogation) from my perspective is a valuable contribution to the understanding of demonic dynamics and deliverance.

> Larson, Bob (1999). *Larson's Book of Spiritual Warfare* [book].

This author's focus on the spiritual struggle from the perspective of Satan, the devil trying to exert legal rights to afflict the human race.

> Most Christians fail to view the battle for souls as a spiritual struggle based on exacting rules of procedure, established at the dawn of creation. The devil is like a lawyer in a cosmic courtroom, arguing his case where God is the judge, eternity is at stake, and the stiffest sentence is banishment forever from the presence of God. (Larson, 1999, p. 318)

According to this author, the spirits of God's saints are protected but the body and soul are vulnerable.

> I have since learned the simple truth that when you belong to God, what Satan cannot invade is your spirit. The moment a person is born into the kingdom of God by faith in Christ (Eph. 2:8-9), the spirit is eternally reborn and belongs to God... However, man is a tripartite being (I Thess. 5:23), and there are aspects of the human condition that Satan can afflict. While he is prohibited from touching the spirit of God's saints, nothing prevents him from tormenting the body and soul – if the disobedient conduct of a Christian allows him to do so. (Larson, 1999, p. 327-328)

One of the author's most significant contributions, as I see it, is the way he attempts to clarify how Satan is attacking the human race.

> MacNutt, Francis, (1995). *Deliverance from Evil Spirits, a Practical Manual* [book].

Francis MacNutt attacks the subject of deliverance from demonic influence from the perspective of experience. It is not his intent to make a scientific contribution, but to offer a handbook on balance and caution. He endeavors to identify the four categories: sin, emotional trauma, demonic, and mental illness from a Biblical perspective. Some have called his approach in this book, "a sorting out process" relative to the four categories of human dysfunction. Although this is not a scientific articulation, psychological concepts are not absent from the dialog. This author also reviews the area of prayer relative to deliverance and denominational comfort level.

> There are many reasons you may feel you cannot pray for deliverance. If you are Roman Catholic or Episcopalian, you probably have the impression that only a priest should do such a thing (a holy priest at that!). And if you belong to a conservative independent Congregation or mainline Protestant demonization, your church leaders may frown on your involvement in deliverance since they may not even believe in the possibility of demonic infestation. Besides all that, if you have seen any movies like *The Exorcist*, you may be scared out of your wits by the prospect of praying for exorcism! But in the Church it has not always been so. (MacNutt, 1995, p. 130)

In my opinion, one of the most significant contributions of this work is the intellectual simplicity, historical insight, and the attention to what I call deliverance basics.

> McAlpine, Thomas H. (1991). *Facing the Powers – What are the options?* [book excerpt]

This author focuses on the principalities and powers in relationship to elements of the dynamics of human society and areas of impact relative to the Christian mission. I was particularly interested in the definitions of the various traditions that the author believes are part of the process of attempting to understand what the scriptures are saying relative to principalities and powers.

> Christians concerned for mission and living in the midst of these upheavals are returning to what Scripture has to say about the principalities and powers. They are doing so within

various traditions. We have summarized [sic] how the Reformed, Anabaptist, third wave, and social science traditions have struggled to understand the role of the principalities and powers in mission. ...

... To review, we have used *Reformed, Anabaptist, third wave* and *social science* as broad types (with the last overlapping the first three):

The Reformed tradition	emphasizes transforming the power mediated by social structures toward greater compatibility with the gospel.
The Anabaptist tradition	emphasizes the freedom given by the gospel over against the power mediated by social structures.
The third wave tradition	emphasizes miraculous divine power in contrast to the power mediated by social structures.
The social science tradition	attempts to relate the biblical language about the powers to models of reality developed by using the social sciences (McAlpine, 1991, p. 75 – 76)

I feel this is a very significant contribution from a context of social science and social structure as opposed to individual deliverance in the spiritual warfare arena.

Mitchell, L. David, (1999). *Liberty in Jesus* [book].

Dr. Mitchell offers insight and interesting information on an area of Christianity often avoided – the understanding of demons. The perspective is from a practical minister who takes God's eternal character seriously. Dr. Mitchell's belief is that deliverance from evil spirits is probably God's answer to healing what may seem to be overpowering (emotional, physical, moral, and mental) conditions; that seem to resist medication, counseling, or prayer. He declares that these problems may be healed by the delivering power revealed by Jesus Christ. "Emotional, moral, mental and sometimes physical conditions which seem unyielding to medicine, counseling [sic] or prayer, may be healed by the delivering power of Christ" (Mitchell, 1999, back cover). "None of these problems are insurmountable. Confession, renunciation and the authoritative prayer of deliverance in the Name of the Lord Jesus Christ will bring liberty and joy as may not have been imagined" (Mitchell, 1999, p.151).

Dr. Mitchell has extensive experience in the area of deliverance ministry. The author points out the need for a Biblical World view of how demons influence and operate in humans. Dr. Mitchell has traced many spheres of influence and activity of demons in some detail. He analyses the issues of spirits, good and evil. This may be his most impactful contribution to the arena. The prayer I will utilize in this study is from this book. The rationalization has been articulated in the Theory/Literature Review chapter.

Monroe, Dr. Myles, (2000). Understanding the Purpose and Power of Prayer, Earthly License for Heavenly Interference [book].

This author concentrates on prayer and believes that prayer is learned and is not an automatic behavior for believers.

When a person becomes a believer, he or she is normally told, "Read the Word, go to church, and pray." Yet many people don't stop to think that these things don't necessarily come naturally to us. We have to learn how to study the Word, How we are meant to function in the body of Christ, and how we are to pray. (Monroe, 2000, p. 117)

This author covers prayer extensively relative to its importance to a grown up, thriving, delivered Christian; in my opinion an invaluable contribution to the field.

Murphy, Dr. Ed, (1996). *The Handbook for Spiritual Warfare* [book].

Dr. Murphy's work may be the most detailed and comprehensive work on spiritual warfare, incorporating theological and psychiatric disciplines, and concepts. His research and experience considers the evil supernatural aspect as well as the elements of mental disorders as potential sources of behavior that fall outside of what society views as normal. From his perspective, there is a fierce conflict between good and evil.

> The kingdom of God and the kingdom of evil supernaturalism are engaged in fierce conflict one against the other. Absolute dualism affirms that ultimate reality is eternally dualistic, that evil and good have always existed, and always will exist. (Murphy, 1996, p.13)

The in-depth scientific methodology of Dr. Murphy's arguments may be his most significant contribution. The detail of his dialog from a World view perspective brings a balance to the argument of demonic influence as opposed to mental destabilization to explain some of the phenomena surrounding the supernatural.

Peck, M.D., M. Scott, (1983). *People of the Lie* [book].

Dr. Peck's perspective is unique because he brings the training of a medical doctor in Behavioral Sciences to the arena of spiritual warfare or spiritual supernatural phenomena.   He applies scientific techniques of psychiatry with an understanding of theologians' skills in what he calls exorcism; he promotes a scientific study, that would examine the phenomenon of possession and exorcism.

> While I have endeavored to my utmost to be objective, the fact remains that the preceding account of two cases of possession and exorcism is a subjective one of my personal experience. I am certain that each team member would write a different tale. I believe that the phenomena of possession and exorcism need to be studied scientifically. It is more than a matter of idle scientific curiosity. While genuine possession

may be a rare phenomenon, the subject represents a veritable untapped gold mine for scientific unearthing. (Peck, 1983, p. 200)

This author takes aim at human evil and the elements of the spiritual supernatural. His most significant contribution may be his scientific perspective with a theological understanding of the supernatural, natural, deliverance and exorcism.

Prince, Derek, (1998). *They Shall Expel Demons* [book].

This author reviews the elements of access and control in the pre and post Christian life. I appreciate his statement on pre-baptism demon affliction.

Let us consider first the case of a person who already has demons when he or she seeks salvation. I have not been able to find any passage of Scripture suggesting that demons will automatically leave at that time. In fact, the ministry of Philip in Samaria suggests the opposite. If the demons left automatically when the people believed and were baptized, why would Philip have spent time and energy driving them out? He could simply have baptized the new believers, which would have eliminated the demons. (Prince, 1998, p. 145)

The pre Christian dialog alone, in my opinion, is a significant contribution to the field.

Robeson, Dr. Jerry & Robeson, Dr. Carol (1997). *Strongman's His Name...II, Biblical Answers to Spiritual Warfare Questions* [book].

Drs. Jerry and Carol Robeson approach the subject of spiritual warfare in their book from a question and answer format. This book is a response to questions generated from their first book on the subject (*Strongman is His Name What's His Game*), as well as lectures. The concentration is on what they call the strongholds of demonic powers, that lord over certain areas, i.e. death, infirmities, etc. Both have ministered for twenty years in Latin America, and understand the issue of spiritual warfare from a Third World context and perspective.

Their approach is straight forward, sometimes controversial, a non-pedantic look at the issue of demons and how they impact human beings, and how they can be confronted. They promote the concept of individuals praying for themselves.

> As the Holy Spirit led us, we developed methods of teaching the new ones to fend for themselves in spiritual matters much sooner than had been the pattern in the past.
>
> For instance, after giving them thorough instruction concerning Divine healing, we would instruct them, "If you get sick, don't call the pastor – you pray for yourselves. Your faith is as effective as ours so just believe what God's Word says and receive it by faith." They were new converts and didn't know any different – so they did it – and were healed! (Robeson & Robeson, 1990, p.1 - 2)

Their most significant contribution may be simplicity without minimizing the significance, and urgency of addressing the demonic realm.

Weber, Stu (2001). *Spirit Warriors* [book].

This author uses militaristic metaphorical language to describe the elements of spiritual warfare.

> Christ is your commander in chief. As a soldier, your life focus is "to please the one who enlisted [you] as a soldier" (2 Timothy 2:4). Paul even came to regard his personal friends not so much as buddies but as soldiers in the same foxhole. They were not his fishing buddies, or business partners, or ministry assistants. They were fellow soldiers. (Philippians 2:25)
>
> Everywhere the New Testament insists the Christian life is about being a faithful warrior. The Christian life is about fighting the good fight, waging war, and wrestling or struggling with a fierce, implacable enemy. The fight of the

Christian man or woman is the life of a spirit warrior. (Weber, 2001, p. 11)

This approach provides a link relating to New Testament soldiering, and may be the most significant contribution the author makes.

Whyte, H. A. Maxwell, (1973). *Casting Out Demons* [book].

This author reveals very directly the demonic conflict relative to the spirit, soul and body of man. But what caught my attention was the author's statement on demonic personalities, and their need to express themselves through a body.

> Demons have distinct and unique personalities, just as human beings do. No two demons are the same. I have seen some highly unusual demonic personalities manifesting themselves through people... It is important to remember that neither Satan nor his demon spirits are "things." Neither can they be taken lightly. Demons are beings having malign intelligence, and each one desires to find a body wherein to express himself. (Whyte, 1973, p. 51-52)

I find the author's discourse on this area alone a significant contribution of insight.

Whyte, H. A. Maxwell, (1989). *Demons & Deliverance.* [book]

In this book Maxwell Whyte expands upon his previous work *Casting Out Demons*, going into more detail in some areas. As I focused on this book, the dialog about healing and deliverance provided an interesting perspective.

> Are healing and deliverance the same? Jesus didn't think so. He distinctly differentiated between divine healing and deliverance from demons. 'And these signs shall follow them that believe; In my name shall they cast out devils; they shall speak with new tongues; They shall take up serpents; and if they drink any deadly thing, it shall not hurt them; they shall

lay hands on the sick, and they shall recover. Mark 16:17-18'
[sic]. The first sign was casting our demons in His name.
(Whyte, 1989, p. 23- 24)

This author points out that deliverance and healing are distinctly
different signs, and implied that deliverance should precede healing.
This contribution to the field strikes me as being controversial but
significant.

Wink, Walter, (1984). *Naming the Powers.* [book]

This author explores the concept of fallen angels, evil spirits and
demons from a perspective of their influencing nations, as well as
individuals. He asserts this evil (that is not of humanity) is not divine but
transcendent, superhuman and opposed to God. The author identifies the
fallen angels, evil spirits and demons as being focused on disrupting human
faithfulness and endeavors to bring destruction, illness, demonization and
death to mankind. He addresses the controversy around the term power
or powers and references ancient texts such as Enoch and Jubilees. The
author asserts that power(s) have duel forms or roles.

Every Power tends to have a visible pole, and outer form – be
it a church, a nation, or an economy – and an invisible pole,
an inner spirit or driving force that animates, legitimates, and
regulates its physical manifestation in the world. Neither pole
is the cause of the other. Both come into existence together and
cease to exist together. When a particular Power becomes
idolatrous, placing itself above God's purposes for the good
of the whole, then that Power becomes demonic. (Wink,
1984, p. 5)

The author's approach to the Old and New Testament in identifying
what he articulates as evil powers is constructed well. The most
important contribution of this offering may be the identification of the
power(s) of the New Testament, and the universal control they may exact
over humanity.

Wink, Walter, (1986). *Unmasking the Powers* [book].

The author addresses the satanic-demonic realm from a spiritual, scientific and academic approach. The author endeavors to demonstrate the span of influence that the supernatural has on the corporate, national, congregational and personal individual levels of our existence.

> The corporate spirits of IBM and Gulf Western are palpably real and striking different, as are the national spirits of the United States and Canada, or the congregational spirits ('angels' or 'demons' were actual entities, only they were not hovering in the air. They were incarnate in cellulose, or cement, or skin and bones, or an empire, or its mercenary armies. (Wink, 1986, p. 4 – 5)

This author's contribution to the arena of deliverance and spiritual warfare in relation to identifying and tracking activity of the principalities and powers is well known and very significant.

> Worley, Win (1976). *Battling the Hosts of Hell– Diary of an Exorcist* [book].

This author articulates his experiences as an exorcist and stresses the concept that the human will cannot be coerced.

> Although believers wielding the name of Jesus have authority over every demon spirit, they cannot coerce the human will. In dealing with individuals Jesus did not violate the human will. We have had cases where deliverance was proceeding smoothly until some spirit (discerned by the workers) was rebuked and commanded to manifest and to leave. When this concerned an area un-surrendered to the Lord, the person immediately emerged and the demon was released from pressure. Deliverance ceased immediately, and most of the time the person became angry and upset. (Worley, 1976, p.126)

Another major insight of this book is what the author calls demonic extremism.

Demons have revealed that they specialize in extremes. It is relatively easy to understand their workings when it comes to evil; however, more obscure and often overlooked is their sinister activity in seizing upon basically good and up-building qualities, driving them to become a compulsive caricature. In this manner, desirable character traits and goals which should be integrating and reinforcing to the person become, instead, disintegrating and weakening factors. (Worley, 1976, p. 236)

I would conclude that the concept of non-coercion of the human will and the insight relative to demonic extremism are valuable contributions to the spiritual warfare arena.

Wylie-Kellermann, Bill (1991). Season of Faith and Conscience: Kairos, Confession, Liturgy [book].

One of the goals the author in this offering, seeks to accomplish is to explain the powers that be, and why the cycle of political resistance has begun to coincide with the liturgical calendar of the church.

That is exactly what this extraordinary book will do. It is exemplary of the kind of biblical work that is reshaping the church and transforming biblical scholarship itself. And it will help to explain to the politicians, military leaders, and magistrates, wise enough to read it, why the cycle of political resistance has begun to coincide with the church's liturgical calendar! (Wylie-Kellerman, 1991, p. xv)

Wylie-Kellerman quoting William Stringfellow points out that principalities, and powers do have some influence through institutions, which include political, military, economic and social, that need to be confronted.

What is most crucial about this situation, biblically speaking, is the failure of moral theology, in the American context, to confront the principalities – the institutions, systems, ideologies, and other political and social powers – as militant, aggressive, and immensely influential creatures in this world as it is. (Wylie-Kellerman, 1991, p. 71)

As far as I am concerned a fresh, bold, and challenging look at the supernatural conflict, and spiritual warfare from more of a liturgical and social conscience impact context; this is a significant and valuable contribution.

Zuendel, Fredrich (2000). *The Awakening* [book].

This book articulates the experiences of a battle between the supernatural and Johann Christopher Blumhardt, a nineteenth century German pastor, still considered a pioneer in the deliverance arena. A comment on the modern mind set of that time, relative to satanic activity, in my opinion is significant for this century.

> Modern minds tend to deny or ignore the very existence of satanic forces, let alone their hold on specific individuals. Blumhardt felt that this skepticism trivializes the reality of evil. He argued that every human being has demons of his or her own to fight, that all are affected in some way by the power of evil.
>
> As soon as one tells a bible [sic] story with a phrase like 'then he cast out the demon....' People tune out; they dismiss it as religious nonsense. They do this because they cannot recognize any capacity for evil, any wretchedness in themselves.
>
> Blumhardt's insights have great relevance today, when interest (and involvement) in pagan religions, the occult, satanism, and New Age philosophy is at an unprecedented high. So does his recognition that in fighting for clarity in any of these areas, scientific or psychological literature is of little help – even if informative, it does not take evil seriously and is therefore unable to inspire action against it. (Zuendel, 2000, p.xvi - xvii)

In my opinion, the insight and information that is presented, is a valuable resource and contribution to the field of knowledge relative to spiritual warfare and deliverance that is still of value today.

Appendix B
Observation Tool and Results

Deliverance Prayer Survey Observation
November 8, 2002

Observer's Name: Freddie

Gender of Participant: Female _____ **Male** ___X___

Observation: ____1____

Eye activity ____X____ (Other Observations) ____

Coughing/Choking_____

Vomiting_____

Throwing up Phlegm_____

Falling to the Floor_____X_____

Noises: _____

Other Body Movements: Knees moved _____

Other Observations: Hands were raised, fists balled, shaking of
fist maintained prayerful position on the floor with eyes closed,
grateful hug at end of prayer

Deliverance Prayer Survey Observation
November 8, 2002

Observer's Name: Freddie

Gender of Participant: Female_____Male__ X____

Observation:_____ 2_____

Eye activity_____ X_____ (Other Body Movements)_____

Coughing/Choking_ X (Tongue out, heavy blowing)_____

Vomiting_____

Throwing up Phlegm _____

Falling to the Floor_____

Noises:___ X (Other Observations)_____

Other Body Movements:_ Hands (arms) raised, eyes closed_____

Other Observations: Heavy breathing, stretching of arms, seemed_ grateful after the prayer_____

Deliverance Prayer Survey Observation
November 8, 2002

Observer's Name: Freddie

Gender of Participant: Female _X_____Male _____

Observation:____3_____

Eye activity_____X_____(Other Observations)___

Coughing/Choking_____

Vomiting_____

Throwing up Phlegm_____

Falling to the Floor_____

Noises:_____

Other Body Movements:_____

Other Observations: Had her hands, eyes closed. Eyes opened, hands on chest, hands are raised, receptive spirit

Deliverance Prayer Survey Observation
November 8, 2002

Observer's Name: Freddie

Gender of Participant: Female___X___Male _____

Observation:_____4_____

Eye activity_____X_____ (Other Observations)___

Coughing/Choking_____

Vomiting_____

Throwing up Phlegm_____

Falling to the Floor_____

Noises:_____

Other Body Movements:_____

Other Observations: Hands raised, eyes closed, moving from side to side, Eye to eye contact made at the end of prayer, smile and gave grateful gesture

Deliverance Prayer Survey Observation
November 8, 2002

Observer's Name: Freddie

Gender of Participant: Female___X___Male _____

Observation:_____5_____

Eye activity_____X_____ (Other Body Movements)_____

Coughing/Choking_____

Vomiting_____

Throwing up Phlegm_____

Falling to the Floor_____X__________

Noises:_____

Other Body Movements: Hands raised, eyes closed_____

Other Observations: Body stretched back_____

Deliverance Prayer Survey Observation
November 8, 2002

Observer's Name: Freddie

Gender of Participant: Female_____Male ____X____

Observation:____6_____

Eye activity_____X_____(Other Observations)____

Coughing/Choking_____

Vomiting_____

Throwing up Phlegm_____

Falling to the Floor_____

Noises:_____

Other Body Movements:___Hands raised_____

Other Observations: Eyes opened, eyes closed, movement of_____
opening and closing of hands, reopened eyes_____

Deliverance Prayer Survey Observation
November 8, 2002

Observer's Name: Freddie

Gender of Participant: Female_____Male ____X____

Observation:____7_____

Eye activity_____X_____ (Other Observations)___

Coughing/Choking_____

Vomiting_____

Throwing up Phlegm_____

Falling to the Floor_____X_____

Noises:_____

Other Body Movements:_____

Other Observations: Eyes Closed_____

Deliverance Prayer Survey Observation
November 8, 2002

Observer's Name: Freddie

Gender of Participant: Female_____Male ____X____

Observation:_____8_____

Eye activity_____X_____(Other Observations)___

Coughing/Choking_____

Vomiting_____

Throwing up Phlegm_____

Falling to the Floor X (Upon the touch fell to the floor)

Noises: _____

Other Body Movements:_____

Other Observations: Eyes Closed_____

Deliverance Prayer Survey Observation
November 8, 2002

Observer's Name: Freddie

Gender of Participant: Female___X___Male _____

Observation:_____9_____

Eye activity_____X_____(Other Body Movements)_____

Coughing/Choking_____

Vomiting_____

Throwing up Phlegm_____

Falling to the Floor_____X__(Other observations)

Noises:_____

Other Body Movements:___Eyes Closed_____

Other Observations: Hands raised, movement of mouth, hands
open and closed, bending of back, hands on knees, strained expression
of face (a prayerful face), leaned forward, fell on knees to floor,
heavy breathing, hugged at end of prayer

Deliverance Prayer Survey Observation
November 8, 2002

Observer's Name: Freddie

Gender of Participant: Female__X__Male _____

Observation:_____10_____

**Eye activity__ X (Other Body Movements-Other Observations)____

Coughing/Choking_____

Vomiting_____

Throwing up Phlegm_____

Falling to the Floor_____

Noises:_____X (Other Observations)_____

Other Body Movements:_____Hands raised, eyes closed_____

Other Observations: Hands raised, eyes closed, hands closed moved from side to side, began to cry, keeps moving back, sniffle, hugged and cried_____

Deliverance Prayer Survey Observation
November 8, 2002

Observer's Name: Edna

Gender of Participant: Female_____Male ____X____

Observation:_____1_____

Eye activity_____X__(Other Body Observations)__

Coughing/Choking_____

Vomiting_____

Throwing up Phlegm_____

Falling to the Floor_____X (in sitting position)___

Noises:_____

Other Body Movements:___Shaking, standing, while constantly bending knees, eyes closed_____

Other Observations:_____

Deliverance Prayer Survey Observation
November 8, 2002

Observer's Name: Edna

Gender of Participant: Female_____Male ____X____

Observation:_____2_____

Eye activity_____X__(Other Body Observations)__

Coughing/Choking__X_____

Vomiting_____

Throwing up Phlegm_____

Falling to the Floor_____

Noises:_____X__(Other Body Movements)_____

Other Body Movements:___Hands raised, eyes closed, heavy breathing hard blowing, speaking, licking tongue out, stretching with hands raised high, squinting, on tip toe_____

Other Observations:_____

Deliverance Prayer Survey Observation
November 8, 2002

Observer's Name: Edna

Gender of Participant: Female___X___Male _____

Observation:____3_____

Eye activity_____X__(Other Body Observations)__

Coughing/Choking_____

Vomiting_____

Throwing up Phlegm_____

Falling to the Floor_____

Noises:_____

Other Body Movements:_ Eyes opened, hands raised, closed eyes tight when hands were placed on chest _____

Other Observations:_____

Deliverance Prayer Survey Observation
November 8, 2002

Observer's Name: Edna

Gender of Participant: Female___X___Male _____

Observation:_____4_____

Eye activity_____ X   (Other Body Observations)__

Coughing/Choking_____

Vomiting_____

Throwing up Phlegm_____

Falling to the Floor_____

Noises:_____

Other Body Movements:___Hands were raised, eyes closed, slow movement from one leg to another_____

Other Observations:_____

Deliverance Prayer Survey Observation
November 8, 2002

Observer's Name: Edna

Gender of Participant: Female___X___Male _____

Observation:_____5_____

Eye activity_____X___(Other Body Movements)___

Coughing/Choking_____

Vomiting_____

Throwing up Phlegm_____

Falling to the Floor_____X_____

Noises:_____

Other Body Movements:__Hands raised, eyes closed, in a daze, jerking, shaking, leaning backwards for a couple of minutes until falling to the floor_____

Other Observations:_____

Deliverance Prayer Survey Observation
November 8, 2002

Observer's Name: Edna

Gender of Participant: Female_____Male ____X____

Observation:_____6_____

Eye activity_____X__(Other Body Movements)____

Coughing/Choking_____

Vomiting_____

Throwing up Phlegm_____

Falling to the Floor_____

Noises:_____X__(Other Body Movements)_____

Other Body Movements:____Eyes opened, saying, "Yes, Lord." hands raised, moving from one leg to another, spoke words with fists balled up, stretching arm, rubbed nose, smiling____

Other Observations:_____

Deliverance Prayer Survey Observation
November 8, 2002

Observer's Name: Edna

Gender of Participant: Female_____Male ____X____

Observation:_____7_____

Eye activity_____ X (Other Body Movements)___

Coughing/Choking_____

Vomiting_____

Throwing up Phlegm_____

Falling to the Floor_____ X_____

Noises:_____

Other Body Movements:__ Eyes closed, hands raised, stomach shaking (popping in and out), leaning backward before actually falling to the floor_____

Other Observations:_____

Deliverance Prayer Survey Observation
November 8, 2002

Observer's Name: Edna

Gender of Participant: Female_____Male _____X_____

Observation:_____8_____

Eye activity_____

Coughing/Choking_____

Vomiting_____

Throwing up Phlegm_____

Falling to the Floor _X (Instantly fell to the floor)_

Noises:_____

Other Body Movements:_____

Other Observations:_____

Deliverance Prayer Survey Observation
November 8, 2002

Observer's Name: Edna

Gender of Participant: Female___X___Male _____

Observation:____9_____

Eye activity_____X___(Other Body Movements)___

Coughing/Choking_____

Vomiting_____

Throwing up Phlegm_____

Falling to the Floor__X_(on knees)_____

Noises:_____X_(Other Body Movements)_____

Other Body Movements: Hands raised, eyes closed, leaning forward, fist closed tight, fingers_ spread open, holding knees, face in the mode for crying, biting lips, falling forward on knees, crawling on knees stood up, arms stretched out

Other Observations:_____

Deliverance Prayer Survey Observation
November 8, 2002

Observer's Name: Edna

Gender of Participant: Female___X___Male _____

Observation:_____10_____

Eye activity_____X__(Other Body Movements)____

Coughing/Choking_____

Vomiting_____

Throwing up Phlegm_____

Falling to the Floor_____

Noises:_____X (Other Body Movements)_____

Other Body Movements: __Eyes closed, hands raised, stomach moving in and out, swelling up for a cry, walking backward, soft balled up fist, fingers spreading open, frowned face, shaking, mouth pushed out, crying, keeps moving back_____

Other Observations:_____

Deliverance Prayer Survey Observation
November 8, 2002

Observer's Name: Elder Steve

Gender of Participant: Female_____Male ___X___

Observation:____1_____

Eye activity_____

Coughing/Choking_____

Vomiting_____

Throwing up Phlegm_____

Falling to the Floor_____X_____

Noises:_____X_(A light moaning)_____

Other Body Movements: His body began to shake_____

Other Observations: After falling to the floor he began to cry and lift up his hands_____

Deliverance Prayer Survey Observation
November 8, 2002

Observer's Name: Elder Steve

Gender of Participant: Female_____Male ____X____

Observation:____2_____

Eye activity_____

Coughing/Choking_____

Vomiting_____

Throwing up Phlegm_____

Falling to the Floor_____X_____

Noises:_____

Other Body Movements: He just stood with his hands lifted up____

Other Observations:_____

Deliverance Prayer Survey Observation
November 8, 2002

Observer's Name: Elder Steve

Gender of Participant: Female___X___Male _____

Observation:_____3_____

Eye activity_____

Coughing/Choking_____

Vomiting_____

Throwing up Phlegm_____

Falling to the Floor_____

Noises:_____

Other Body Movements:_____

Other Observations: There appeared to be a peace that came over her as she stood still_____

Deliverance Prayer Survey Observation
November 8, 2002

Observer's Name: Elder Steve

Gender of Participant: Female____X____Male _____

Observation: _____4_____

Eye activity _____X_(Other Observations)

Coughing/Choking_____

Vomiting_____

Throwing up Phlegm_____

Falling to the Floor_____

Noises:_____X (A light whisper)_____

Other Body Movements: _Swaying back and forth_____

Other Observations: There was a straight staring look on her face after a few moments she began to smile_____

Deliverance Prayer Survey Observation
November 8, 2002

Observer's Name: Elder Steve

Gender of Participant: Female___X___Male _____

Observation:_____5_____

Eye activity_____

Coughing/Choking_____

Vomiting_____

Throwing up Phlegm_____

Falling to the Floor_____X_____

Noises:_____

Other Body Movements:_____

Other Observations:_____

Deliverance Prayer Survey Observation
November 8, 2002

Observer's Name: Elder Steve

Gender of Participant: Female_____Male ____X____

Observation: _____6_____

Eye activity_____X_(Other Body Movements)____

Coughing/Choking_____

Vomiting_____

Throwing up Phlegm_____

Falling to the Floor_____X_____

Noises:_____

Other Body Movements:_____

Other Observations: After having his eyes closed, he opened them and began staring back

Deliverance Prayer Survey Observation
November 8, 2002

Observer's Name: Elder Steve

Gender of Participant: Female_____Male _____X_____

Observation:_____7_____

Eye activity_____

Coughing/Choking_____X_____

Vomiting_____

Throwing up Phlegm_____

Falling to the Floor_____X_____

Noises:_____X (Began to groan)_____

Other Body Movements: Swaying back and forth_____

Other Observations: He began to move as though something was pushing from the inside out and his stomach started to flutter and he tried to walk backward_____

Deliverance Prayer Survey Observation
November 8, 2002

Observer's Name: Elder Steve

Gender of Participant: Female_____Male ___X___

Observation:_____8_____

Eye activity_____

Coughing/Choking_____

Vomiting_____

Throwing up Phlegm_____

Falling to the Floor_____X_____

Noises:_____

Other Body Movements:_____

Other Observations: As he walked up for prayer, as soon as he was touched he fell to the ground

Deliverance Prayer Survey Observation
November 8, 2002

Observer's Name: Elder Steve

Gender of Participant: Female___X___Male _____

Observation:_____9_____

Eye activity_____

Coughing/Choking_____

Vomiting_____

Throwing up Phlegm_____

Falling to the Floor_____X_____

Noises:_____X_(Other Observations)_____

Other Body Movements: Her body began to jerk and bend over.

Other Observations: She started to cry and make expressions of pain. She fell to her knees and moved as though something was pushing her back and forth

Deliverance Prayer Survey Observation
November 8, 2002

Observer's Name: Elder Steve

Gender of Participant: Female___X___Male _____

Observation:_____10_____

Eye activity_____

Coughing/Choking_____

Vomiting_____

Throwing up Phlegm_____

Falling to the Floor_____

Noises:_____X (Other Observations)_____

Other Body Movements: Swaying back and forth, hands shaking

Other Observations: She began to cry, and moved back like she was trying to get away

Deliverance Prayer Survey Observation
November 8, 2002

Observer's Name: Denise

Gender of Participant: Female_____Male ___X___

Observation:_____1_____

Eye activity_____

Coughing/Choking_____

Vomiting_____

Throwing up Phlegm_____

Falling to the Floor X (Other Body Movement)

Noises:_____

Other Body Movements: Slight shaking, leaned backwards, knees bending, some bouncing; bent back and fell backward on his bottom in a praying position_____

Other Observations:_____

Deliverance Prayer Survey Observation
November 8, 2002

Observer's Name: Denise

Gender of Participant: Female_____Male ____X____

Observation: ____2_____

Eye activity_____X_(closed)_____

Coughing/Choking____X_____

Vomiting_____

Throwing up Phlegm_____

Falling to the Floor_____

Noises: X (Other Body Movements-Other Observations)

Other Body Movements: Leaned backwards, appeared out of breath, breathing hard, sweating, panting, panting, reaching high, exhaling leaned backward

Other Observations: A calmness after exhaling

Deliverance Prayer Survey Observation
November 8, 2002

Observer's Name: Denise

Gender of Participant: Female ___X___ Male _____

Observation: ____3_____

Eye activity _____X__ (Other Observations) _____

Coughing/Choking _____

Vomiting _____

Throwing up Phlegm _____

Falling to the Floor _____

Noises: _____

Other Body Movements: _____ _____

Other Observations: Eyes opened and closed, opened and closed_

Deliverance Prayer Survey Observation
November 8, 2002

Observer's Name: Denise

Gender of Participant: Female____X____Male _____

Observation:_____4_____

No observation notes

Eye activity_____

Coughing/Choking_____

Vomiting_____

Throwing up Phlegm_____

Falling to the Floor_____

Noises: _____

Other Body Movements:_____

Other Observations:_____No Data_____

Deliverance Prayer Survey Observation
November 8, 2002

Observer's Name: Denise

Gender of Participant: Female____X____Male _____

Observation:_____5_____

Eye activity_____

Coughing/Choking_____

Vomiting_____

Throwing up Phlegm_____

Falling to the Floor_X (Other Observations)_____

Noises:_____

Other Body Movements:_____

Other Observations: Shaking, leans backward, laid on the floor – very still _____

Deliverance Prayer Survey Observation
November 8, 2002

Observer's Name: Denise

Gender of Participant: Female_____Male ___X___

Observation:____6_____

Eye activity_____X (Other Observations)_____

Coughing/Choking_____

Vomiting_____

Throwing up Phlegm_____

Falling to the Floor _X (Other Observations)_____

Noises: _____

Other Body Movements:_____

Other Observations: Very focused on every word, direct eye contact, no blinking, eyes slowly closed. Fell to ground, laid on floor backward

Deliverance Prayer Survey Observation
November 8, 2002

Observer's Name: Denise

Gender of Participant: Female_____Male ___X___

Observation:_____7_____

Eye activity_____

Coughing/Choking_____

Vomiting_____

Throwing up Phlegm_____

Falling to the Floor X (Other Observations)_____

Noises: ___X (Other Observations)_____

Other Body Movements:_____

Other Observations: Giggling in the stomach. Jumping in the stomach. Fell backwards_____

Deliverance Prayer Survey Observation
November 8, 2002

Observer's Name: Denise

Gender of Participant: Female_____Male ____X____

Observation:_____8_____

Eye activity_____

Coughing/Choking_____

Vomiting_____

Throwing up Phlegm_____

Falling to the Floor _X_ (Other Observations)_____

Noises:_____

Other Body Movements:_____

Other Observations: I missed this person. I looked up and he was down on the floor_____

Deliverance Prayer Survey Observation
November 8, 2002

Observer's Name: Denise

Gender of Participant: Female___X___Male _____

Observation:_____9_____

Eye activity_____

Coughing/Choking_____

Vomiting_____

Throwing up Phlegm_____

Falling to the Floor X (Other Observations)_____

Noises: X (Other Observations)_____

Other Body Movements:_____

Other Observations: Bent over; crying, annoying facial expression; squatted on floor; crawling; stood tall – suddenly

Deliverance Prayer Survey Observation
November 8, 2002

Observer's Name: Denise

Gender of Participant: Female__ X __Male _____

Observation:____10____

Eye activity_____X__(Other Observations)_____

Coughing/Choking_____

Vomiting_____

Throwing up Phlegm_____

Falling to the Floor_____

Noises:__X__(Other Observations)_____

Other Body Movements:_____

Other Observations: Swaying, stepped backwards, balled up fist, slowly. Opening and closing mouth, frowning, slight shaking, crying, dripping tears, swaying and stepping backwards

Appendix C
Participants Question Response Form

A brief interview of the participants was conducted by Denise one of the observers. The interview went as follows: "You know that was Dr. Maddox praying for you? He has asked me to ask you a question, is that all right with you? The question is, "What did you experience?"

Participant #1 Male

"I felt free like a bird." "It's like I could forget my past." "Light headed." "Good." "Can't express…It's the peace…I've been searching for."

Participant #2 Male

"Like a backward pull." "As he was calling out, it was pulling from within." "I've had problems with my bowels, but I felt the peace of God there." "I have gone to many Deliverances, but always left with some feeling of freedom, but tonight I felt total freedom." "I always felt there is a point that the demons would come out, but the doctor (Maddox) knew that they were there and made them come out." "Praise God!"

Participant #3 Female

No interview notes, someone else finished praying for this person.

Participant #4 Female

"I was very uncomfortable, probably because I'm pregnant,(due 12/16)." "I felt the anointing, peace." " A clearer conscious." "All worries just feels gone." "He's a good teacher." "Very powerful and anointed." (She had a big smile through the interview.)

Participant #5 Female

"I've been prayed for before but when Dr. Maddox prayed, I really sensed in my spirit that God was involved." "It's a difference." "A very high anointing." "A lot of things he said related back to my past that he couldn't know about or what I had been through."

Participant #6 Male

"Felt good." "… Like something is going to happen." "Dr. Maddox spoke to my situation without knowing what it was but I knew what he was talking about." "Felt like God was doing something in me while I was laying down."

Participant #7 Male

"A real calm and peace." "The things that he spoke, he spoke quietly, like it was a private conversation, but I heard it amplified." "When I was on the floor, the Lord was showing things from the past to me real clear. I knew he was not going to let me go back."

Participant #8 Male

"He didn't even begin praying." "I don't know what happened and all of a sudden I was encompassed by the spirit and was slayed under. I guess God was doing his thing." "Felt like an invasion," "Overpowered." "My thoughts were wiped out, I was going to ask from prayers for my new position at church. I wanted to ask for success and to live up to the responsibility…but everything happened so fast."

Participant #9 Female

"Very refreshed and encouraged." "Felt the presence of God, like an assurance, then empowered." "Warm sensation." "Safe/secure." "Knowing that truth is being applied into your spirit…you can sense it like something was standing next to you and got inside of you, which was Jesus Christ." "Felt the warm power of God coming out of him [Dr. Maddox] into me. I wanted to stay there at that warm place."

Participant #10 Female

"At one point I felt a lot of pain in my feet 1st time that has happened to me." "I was between the feeling of peace and pain in my feet." "I could hear and understand everything he said." "Felt real tired and peaceful." "Feet hurt a little, still; probably from standing so long.

Appendix D

Observation Tool Consolidation Chart

	Gender	Eye Activity	Coughing/ Choking	Falling to the Floor	Noises	Other Body Movements (OBM)	Other Observations (OO)
0							
1	Male	F - (OO) E - (OBM)		F E - In sitting position ES D - (OBM)	ES – A light moaning	F - Knees moved E - Shaking, standing, while constantly bending knees, eyes closed. ES - His body began to shake D - Slight shaking, leaned backwards, knees bending, some bouncing; bent back and fell backward on his bottom in a praying position	F - Hands were raised, fists balled, shaking of fist, maintained prayerful position on the floor with eyes closed, grateful hug at end of prayer ES - After falling to the floor he began to cry and lift up his hands.
2	Male	F - (OBM) E - (OBM) D – Closed	F –Tongue out, heavy blowing E D	ES	**F - (OO)** E - (OBM) D - (OBM – OO)	F - Hands (arms) raised, eyes closed E - Hands raised, eyes closed, heavy breathing, hard blowing, speaking, licking tongue out, stretching with hands raised high, squinting, on tip toe. ES - He just stood with his hands lifted up D - Leaned backwards, appeared out of breath, breathing hard, sweating, panting, reaching high, exhaling leaned backward	F - Heavy breathing, stretching of arms, seemed grateful after the prayer D - A calmness after exhaling

Impact of A Deliverance Prayer

O	Gender	Eye Activity	Coughing/ Choking	Falling to the Floor	Noises	Other Body Movements (OBM)	Other Observations (OO)
3	Female	F - (OO) E - (OBM) D - (OO)				E - Eyes opened, hands raised, closed opened, hands on chest, hands are raised, receptive spirit.	F - Had her hands, eyes closed. Eyes opened, hands on chest, hands are raised, receptive spirit. ES - There appeared to be a peace that came over her as she stood still. D - Eyes opened and closed. Opened and closed.
4	Female	F - (OO) E - (OBM) ES - (OO)			ES – A light whisper	E - Hands were raised, eyes closed, slow movement from one leg to another. ES – Swaying back and forth	F - Hands raised, eyes closed, moving from side to side. Eye to eye contact made at the end of the prayer, smile and gave grateful gesture. ES – There was a straight staring look on her face after a few moments she began to smile.
5	Female	F - (OBM) E - (OBM)		F E ES D (OO)		F - Hands raised, eyes closed E - Hands raised, eyes closed, in a daze, jerking, shaking, leaning backwards for a couple of minutes until falling to the floor	F - Body stretched back. D – Shaking, leans backward, laid on floor – very still.
6	Male	F - (OO) E - (OBM) ES - (OBM) D - (OO)		ES D (OO)	E – (OBM)	F – Hands raised E – Eyes opened, saying, "Yes, Lord," hands raised, moving from one leg to another, spoke words with fists balled up, stretching arm, rubbed nose, smiling	F - Eyes opened, eyes closed, movement of opening and closing of hands, reopened eyes. ES – After having his eyes closed, he opened them and began staring back D – Very focused on every word, direct eye contact, no blinking, eyes slowly closed. Fell to ground, laid on floor backward.

O	Gender	Eye Activity	Coughing/Choking	Falling to the Floor	Noises	Other Body Movements (OBM)	Other Observations (OO)
7	Male	F – (OO) E – (OBM)	ES	F E ES D – (OO)	ES – E – Began to groan D – (OO)	E – Eyes closed, hands raised, stomach shaking (popping in and out), leaning backward before actually falling to the floor. ES – Swaying back and forth	F – Eyes closed ES – He began to move as though something was pushing from the inside out and his stomach started to flutter and he tried to walk backward. D – Giggling in the stomach. Jumping in the stomach. Fell backwards.
8	Male	F – (OO)		F – Upon the touch fell to the floor E – Instantly fell to the floor ES D – (OO)			F – Eyes closed ES – As he walked up for prayer, as soon as he was touched he fell to the ground. D – I missed this person. I looked up and he was down on the floor.
9	Female	F – (OBM) E – (OBM)		F – (OO) E – On knees ES – (OO) D – (OO)	E – (OBM) ES – (OO) D – (OO)	F – Eyes closed E – Hands raised, eyes closed, leaning forward, fist closed tight, fingers spread open, Holding knees, face in the mode for crying, biting lips, falling forward on knees, crawling on knees stood up, arms stretched out. ES –. Her body began to jerk and bend over.	F – Hands raised, movement of mouth, hands opened and closed, bending of back, hands on knees, strained expression of face (a prayerful face), leaned forward, fell on knees to floor, heavy breathing, hugged at end of the prayer, teared. ES – She started to cry and made expressions of pain. She fell to her knees and moved as though something was pushing her back and forth. D – Bent over; crying, annoying facial expression squatted on floor; crawling stood tall – suddenly.

Impact of A Deliverance Prayer

O	Gender	Eye Activity	Coughing/Choking	Falling to the Floor	Noises	Other Body Movements (OBM)	Other Observations (OO)
10	Female	F – (OBM-OO) E – (OBM) D – (OO)			F – (OO) E – (OBM) ES – (OO) D – (OO)	F – Hands raised, eyes closed E – Eyes closed, hands raised, stomach moving in and out, swelling up for a cry, walking backward, soft balled up fist, fingers spreading open, frowned face, shaking mouth pushed out, crying, keeps moving back. ES – Swaying back and forth, hands shaking	F – Hands raised, eyes closed, hands closed moved from side to side, began to cry, keeps moving back, sniffle, hugged and cried. ES – She began to cry, and moved back like she was trying to get away. D – Swaying, stepped backwards, balled up fist slowly. Opening and closing mouth, frowning, slight shaking, crying, dripping tears, swaying and stepping backwards.

Key:
F – Freddie
E – Edna
ES – Elder Steve
D – Denise
O – Observation Number
OBM – Other Body Movements
OO – Other Observations

Appendix E
Post Ministry Event-Impact Interview Form

March 25, 2003

Gender of Participate: ___Female___
Observation: ___4___

Questions and Responses

1. **Why did you come forth for deliverance prayer?**

   Response: "I do not remember."

2. **Had you had deliverance prayer before?**

   Response: "Yes."

3. **What has happened in the way of on going deliverance as a result of the November 8, 2002, prayer?**

   Response: "What was said came to pass, depression was lifted."

4. **Did this particular deliverance prayer make a difference?**

   Response: "Felt the same as other deliverance prayers. God is the one doing the work."

Gender of Participate: __Male__
Observation: ____8____

Questions and Responses

> **1. Why did you come forth for deliverance prayer?**
>
> Response: "Dealing with issues, mostly lusts of the eyes and flesh."

> **2. Had you had deliverance prayer before?**
>
> Response: "Yes."

> **3. What has happened in the way of on going deliverance as a result of the November 8, 2002, prayer?**
>
> Response: "I look at women differently with more respect."

> **4. Did this particular deliverance prayer make a difference?**
>
> Response: "Yes, it did."

Gender of Participate:___Female___
Observation:___9___

Questions and Responses

   1. **Why did you come forth for deliverance prayer?**

      Response: "I needed deliverance from grief-heaviness as a result of my son's death."

   2. **Had you had deliverance prayer before?**

      Response: "Yes."

   3. **What has happened in the way of on going deliverance as a result of the November 8, 2002, prayer?**

      Response: "Freedom from over burden of grief-heaviness."

   4. **Did this particular deliverance prayer make a difference?**

      Response: "Yes, I feel empowered and delivered!"

Gender of Participate: __Female__
Observation: _____10_____

Questions and Responses

    1. Why did you come forth for deliverance prayer?

        Response: "I had a great deal of anger."

    2. Had you had deliverance prayer before?

        Response: "Yes."

    3. What has happened in the way of on going deliverance as a result of the November 8, 2002 prayer?

        Response: "I was delivered from demonic anger, and now can recognize it and bind it when it rises. I can ask myself why the anger is there. I could not do this before."

    4. Did this particular deliverance prayer make a difference?

        Response: "Yes, I got in touch with the Spirit. I can recognize demonic anger when it comes up."

Appendix F
Definitions - Terminology

The definition and terminology sections' goal is to provide some basic background relative to definitions and terminology. Some basic working definitions and terms will be provided by authors and practitioners who operate in the spiritual warfare arena. I will also utilize the *Interpreter's Dictionary of the Bible* as an additional academic resource. The term "working definition" is not to imply the absence of academic foundation, as well; academic definition does not imply the absence of a practical application foundation. History and time have a way of impacting use and meaning relative to definition and terminology.

Terminology

Because of the weaknesses in how some English versions of the Bible translates original Greek texts some meanings have been obscured or misunderstood, creating some problems with meaning relative to describing evil spirits, demonization, and possession.

> Three expressions are used to describe the evil spirit beings who are some of Satan's main agents in his warfare against humanity. First, demon (Greek, *daimonion*). This is the neuter singular of the adjective *daimonios*, which is derived from the noun *daimon*. Thus the adjective *daimonios* indicates some connection with a *daimon*. Although *daimonion* is adjectival in form, it is used regularly as a noun. It is, in fact, an adjective that has become a noun. ... The reference to the original Greek indicates that there are two distinct entities: *daimon*, which is primary, and *daimonion*, which is derivative. (Prince, 1998, p. 14 –15)

A basic understanding of these expressions provides some insight into the controversy. The second and third expressions also provide some revelation to the confusion relative to terminology.

> The second expression used in the New Testament to describe an evil spirit is unclean spirit, used about twenty times in Luke, Acts and Revelation.
>
> The third expression, evil spirit, is used six times in Luke and Acts.
>
> In Luke 4:33 two of these expressions are combined as the writer speaks of "a spirit of an unclean demon" (daimonion).
>
> Altogether it seems that all three expressions are used interchangeably. "Demons" are "unclean spirits" and also "evil spirits."
>
> The original King James Version regularly translates daimonion as "devil." This has led to endless confusion. The English word devil is actually derived from the Greek word diabolos means "slanderer. In all but three occurrences in the New Testament, it is a title of Satan himself. In this sense it is used only in the singular form. There are many demons but only one devil. (Prince, 1998, p. 15)

This terminology confusion is one of the main reasons a controversy surrounds possession and demonization in the deliverance ministry/spiritual warfare arena.

Academic Definitions

The resource for this section is The Interpreter's Dictionary of the Bible (1962) The following abbreviations will appear throughout the definitions:

OT = Old Testament   **NT = New Testament**

Anoint - To smear or pour oil or ointment on the head or body of a person or on an object. This custom, with secular or religious connotation, appears throughout the whole biblical period, both inside and outside Israel. (Buttrick, et al., p. 138)

Anointed, The – In the OT, the designation of the king of Israel and later of the high priest as the high official consecrated by the anointing ...: in post-OT times, the title of the ultimate king, for which, however, the untranslated Aramaic or Greek forms of the word... 'Messiah,' and ...
'Christ,' are better known. (Buttrick, et al., p.139 - 140)

Anointing Oil – Perhaps the most frequent use of oil mentioned in the Bible is that of anointing. Most familiar is the custom of anointing a king. (Buttrick, et al., p. 592)

Binding and Loosing – The power of binding and loosing was entrusted to Peter by Jesus: 'I will give you the keys of the kingdom of heaven, and whatever you bind on earth shall be bound in heaven, whatever you loose on earth shall be loosed in heaven.' (Matt. 16 – 29) ... A parallel to the saying on binding and loosing is found in the words addressed by Jesus to the apostles on the eve of the Resurrection: 'If you forgive the sins of any, they are forgiven; if you retain the sins of any, they are retained; (John 20:23) (Buttrick, et al., p. 438)

Deliverer – The principle theme of the Bible is God's deliverance of mankind from the power of sin, death, and Satan through his action in Jesus Christ; and this mighty deliverance is foreshadowed in the history of God's people

Israel by his deliverance of them from such disasters as Egyptian bondage or Babylonian exile.

...The word 'deliverer' occurs nine times in the OT. ...In the NT, Jesus is never called 'deliverer' or 'redeemer.' In Acts 7:35, Moses is called the 'deliverer.' The Greek word is... 'ransomer,' 'redeemer,' 'liberator', and this is its only occurrence in the NT. In Rom. 11:26, Paul quotes from Isa. 59:20: 'The Deliverer will come from Zion.'... (Buttrick, et al., p. 814 - 815)

Demon – In the original sense, a demon may be defined broadly as an anonymous god – i.e., as a personification of one or another of those vaguer, less identifiable powers and influences that were believed to operate alongside the major deities and to condition particular circumstances and experiences. (Buttrick, et al., p. 817)

Demoniacal Possession – From the standpoint of religious psychology, daimonism represents an externalization of human experiences. Feelings and sensations, moods and impulses, even physical conditions, which might otherwise be described as obtaining autonomously within a man, are portrayed, on this basis, as outer forces working upon him. (Buttrick, et al., p. 818)

Devil – The OT term has its origin in Hebrew judicial terminology as the 'adversary.' In the NT the term ... is understood as the singular and supernatural adversary of God, the tempter and seducer of men. (Buttrick, et al., p.838)

Exorcism - To bind with an oath, to conjure; Exorcist - The practice of expelling evil spirits from persons or places by means of incantations and the performance of certain occult acts. ... In the NT evil and unclean spirits are reported to have been exorcised by Jesus and the disciples without recourse to incantations or occult performances. Jesus cast out demons by the 'Spirit of God' (Matt. 12:28), and by his own word (Matt. 8:16; Mark 1:25; 5:8; 9:25; etc.). This power to drive out spirits was bestowed by Jesus upon his disciples (Matt.

10:1; Mark 6:7), and they accomplished the charge by invoking his name. (Mark 16:17; Acts 16:18; ect.) (Buttrick, et al., p. 199)

Hands, Laying on of – A ceremony occurring in both the OT and the NT in various contexts and meanings. ... In the NT ordination has the same sense. ... In the Pastorals, however, the laying on of hands in ordination is associated with the imparting of a spiritual gift. ... Thus in later church usage, one finds a variety of associations of the ceremony: confirmation, ordination, healing, reconciling penitents, and the imparting of blessings upon both persons and objects. (Buttrick, et al., p.521 - 522)

Healing – The restoration of the sick formed part of subsequent apostolic practice, in conformity with the expressed will of Christ. In the days immediately after Pentecost many healings took place at the hands of the apostles. (Acts 2:43; 5:12; 8:7) (Buttrick, et al., p.547 - 548)

Holy Spirit – The mysterious power of God, conceived in the first place as the mode of God's activity, manifested especially in supernatural revelation to selected individuals and in their being possessed by a force which gave them marvelous strength, courage, wisdom, and the knowledge of God's will and his dealings with men. (Buttrick, et al., p. 626)

Prayer – In the Bible prayer moves from the level of magic to the heights of spiritual communion and identification of will and activity with God. No definition which would cover all the references is possible except in general terms. (Buttrick, et al., p. 857)

Satan - The archfiend, chief of the devils; instigator of all evil; the rival of God; the Antichrist... Meaning of the term. The Hebrew root... from which the name Satan derives, means primarily 'obstruct, oppose'. It is used in the OT of obstructing a man's path. (Buttrick, et al., p. 224)

Spiritual Gifts – The term used in the NT to designate the special endowments of the Member of the church for its service. The gospel of salvation first declared by Jesus, then proclaimed by those who had received it, has been confirmed by God himself 'by signs and wonders and various miracles and by gifts of the Holy Spirit distributed according to his own will' (Heb. 2:4). Such phenomena are called 'spiritual gifts.' (Buttrick, et al., p. 435)

Working Definitions

Anoint - "The Greek word *chrisma** is translated by 'anointing' or 'unction,' and it Means 'a rubbing in or spreading on of oil." (Holdcroft, 1979, p. 87)

Anointed One - 'The object being anointed. The more common Old Testament word comes from the noun Messiah, the 'anointed One. One of the three Greek words used is related to the title Christ, the counterpart of Messiah" (Ryrie, 1997. p. 175)

Anointing Oil - 'The Holy Spirit is particularly set forth under the figure of anointing oil in His relationship to Jesus Christ. "Therefore God, even thy God, hath anointed thee with the oil of gladness above thy fellows." (Hebrews 1:9)" (Holdcroft, 1979, p. 30)

Binding - Binding means to bind, gird, wrap around, fetter, tie, press, compress, bind a conspirator, entangle, yoke, fasten…. We are commanded to bind the forces of evil from ourselves and others. We cannot destroy the works of Satan unless we use the weapons of God: binding, loosing and agreeing… (Moody, 1998, p. 347)

Deliverance - 'Deliverance' means 'the act of expelling evil spirits or demons by adjuration in the Name of Jesus Christ and through his power' (Burgess 1988, 290). In the first act of deliverance ministry recorded in Mark, Jesus commands the unclean spirit, 'come out of him' (Mark 1:25). The term 'exorcism' as a synonym of 'deliverance' is found historically in Christianity up to modern times (Cross, 1958, 485 [sic]). (Mitchell, 1999, p. 175)

Deliverance Prayer - The first thing to realize when we are performing a deliverance is that deliverance prayer is different from prayer for healing. In fact, it is not prayer at all; it is a command. And it is directed not to God, as prayer is, but to an evil spirit, ordering it to get out. (MacNutt, 1995, p. 167)

Deliverance Ministry – 'Deliverance ministry includes counselling, discerning of spirits and understanding Satanic influence. Deliverance ministry deals with the breaking of spiritual bondage and culminates in the individual's freedom from the evil spirit(s). (Dickason 1987; Unger 1991; Warner 1991; White 1990; and others. [sic]"). (Mitchell, 1999, p. 176)

Demonization or Demonized – "Demonization' is a noun derived from 'demonized.' Is a personal relationship; the imposition of an evil spirit into the life of a human being' (Wagner and Pennoyer 1990, 250)." (Mitchell, 1999, p. 177)

Demon Manifestations - "When demons are confronted and pressured through spiritual warfare they will sometimes demonstrate their particular natures through the person in a variety of ways. These evil spirits are creatures of darkness." (Hammond & Hammond, 1973, p. 47)

Demons/Evil Spirits - I describe demons as disembodied spirit beings that have an intense craving to occupy physical bodies. Apparently their first choice is a human body; but rather than remain in a disembodied condition, they are willing to enter even the body of an animal (see Luke 8:32 – 33).

It is hard for us to entertain the idea of a person without a body. Nevertheless, even though demons have no bodies, they have all the normally accepted marks of personality:

1. Will
2. Emotion

3. Intellect
4. Self-awareness
5. Ability to speak   (Prince, 1998, p. 89)

The terms 'demons' and 'evil spirits' describe 'divinely created supernatural beings' who, with their leader Satan, rebelled against God (Elwell 1988, 610). Demons have always been thought by many to be 'fallen angels' (ibid., Dickason 1987, 24). Satan uses demons as emissaries for promoting his design to thwart God's plans. (Mitchell, 1999, p. 176)

Devil or Demon Possession – The term 'demon possessed' is commonly used to describe a person with demons living inside.'… 'The term "demon possession" does not appear in the Bible. Apparently it originated with the Jewish historian, Flavius Josephus, in the first century A.D. and then passed into ecclesiastical language." (Kraft, 1992, p. 35 - 36)

Discernment - "Discernment is another way of expressing to 'look beneath the surface' to 'distinguish between spirits' (I Cor. 12:10). Discernment is 'the ability to know the spirits that are from God and those that are evil' Southard 1986, 133)." (Mitchell, 1999, p.178)

Exorcism - The Greek verb that usually describes the action of getting rid of a demon is *ekballo*, normally translated "to drive out," but in the KJV regularly translated "to cast out."… Another Greek verb used in this connection is *exorkizo* normally translated "to exorcise." …In contemporary English, to exorcise is defined as 'to expel evil spirits from a person or a place by prayers, adjurations and religious rites.' The word is used frequently in the rituals of liturgical churches but occurs only once in the New Testament. (Prince, 1998, p. 17)

Experimental Design - Single-case experimental designs used in social science research are typically single-subject designs. That is, only one subject is studied at a time. If more than one subject is involved, the results from the additional subjects are considered replication of the experiment; data on different subjects are rarely combined. However, in some cases the relevant case is a group, not an individual or a series of individuals. (Slavin, 1992, p. 44)

Fruit of the Spirit - "The nine *fruits* of the Spirit, which are a result of the Holy Spirit's *indwelling* Presence." (Hagin, 1997, p. 25)

Gifts of the Spirit – "The nine gifts of the Spirit, which are a result of the Holy Spirit's *infilling* power." (Hagin, 1997, p. 25)

Healing Prayer – "Healing prayer… is directed to God. We certainly do not command God to do anything; we only ask Him – in this case to heal." (MacNutt, 1995, p. 167)

Holy Spirit – 'The Holy Spirit is that Person of the holy Trinity whose office it is to touch upon the believer. He is God communicating himself' (Holdcroft, 1979, p. 5). "The Holy Spirit is the executive or active agent of the Godhead." (Holdcroft, 1979, p. 58)

Holy Spirit Anointing – The New Testament references recall The Old Testament procedure of pouring oil on candidates for appointment as prophet, priest, or king. In the Church, the Holy Spirit anoints every believer for all three of these offices. John wrote: 'Ye have an unction [*chrisma*] from the Holy One. … But the anointing [chrisma] which ye have received of him abideth in you' (I John 2:20, 27). According to John, the Holy Spirit's anointing. (Holdcroft, 1979, p. 87)

Inner Healing – "Inner Healing is a form of Christian counseling and prayer which focuses the healing power of the Spirit on certain types of emotional/spiritual problems." (Kraft, 1992, p. 142)

Intercession – But believers should also see themselves as intercessors: standing between God and the person(s) for whom they are praying, pleading for God to intervene. We also stand between Satan and that person, battling and pushing back the powers of darkness. (Sherrer & Garlock, 1992, p. 224)

Intercessor – "The Hebrew root word for intercessor or intercession is *paga* (paw-gah), meaning "to come between, to assail, to cause to entreat." (Sherrer & Garlock, 1992, p. 224)

Intercessory Prayer – "It is not quick, instant prayer, but continuous, prevailing intercession. It is not one man, a spiritual lone ranger, praying alone, but groups of intercessors, thousands of miles away, who join him in persistent, systematic prayer." (Murphy, 1996, p. 415)

Laying on of Hands – "A powerful spiritual experience, a temporary interaction between two spirits through which supernatural power is released." (Prince, 1998, p.109)

Loosing (Loose) – Means to draw off, cast off, loose, shake off, open, loose off or away, make inactive, send again or up, let go… loose cords on us of affliction or death…the bands of wickedness and get rid of heavy burdens. (Moody, 1998, p. 347)

Open Ended Questions/ Interview – Another common tool of qualitative research is the open-ended interview. … It attempts to let the person being interviewed tell his or her story, respond at length, and lead the interview in directions other than those anticipated by the researcher. Qualitative interviewers usually have some questions prepared and know what information they want by the end of the session, but they may not structure the interview beyond this. (Slavin, 1992, p. 69–70)

Participant Observation – "Whenever the observer interacts with the people being observed, this is called *participant observation*. In contrast, in *nonparticipant observation*, the observer tries to interact as little as possible." (Slavin, 1992, p. 68)

Qualitative Research - Qualitative research (also known as ethnographic or naturalistic research) is research intended to explore important social phenomena by immersing the investigator in the situation for extended periods. ... In general, the qualitative researcher begins with an open mind and, at most, a few hunches about what he or she may see, and starts without a full-blown plan. ... The product of a qualitative study is a thick description, not a report with tables and figures. (Slavin, 1992, p. 65)

Quantitative Research – Collects numerical data from individuals or groups and usually subjects them to statistical analyses to determine whether there are relationships among them. Quantitative research usually poses hypotheses that are either supported or disconfirmed by the data. (Slavin, 1992, p. 11)

Random Sampling/Assignment – "One very important aspect of research design, especially in survey research, is determination of the appropriate sample. As the word implies, a sample is a part of a larger whole." (Slavin, 1992, p.95)

"If students are randomly assigned to treatments, the experimenter determines which students will be in which treatments by a chance process. For example, flipping a coin." (Slavin, 1992, p. 17)

Satan – "The Bible refers to him as Satan, Lucifer, and the devil, progenitor of pride, instigator of avarice, font of folly, source of seduction, origin of temptation, and evocuator of evil." (Larson, 1999, p.38)

Slain (or Slaying) in the Spirit – "Slaying in the Spirit' ... this curious phenomenon, of how people were touched by persons who had this power and just fell over 'under the power." (MacNutt, 1977, p. 189)

Spiritual Warfare – "Spiritual warfare defined throughout this book refers both to the believer's multidimensional war against personal sin and to warfare with Satan and his fallen angels." (Murphy, 1996, p. 521)

Spiritual Warrior – "The Christian life is about fighting the good fight, waging war, and wrestling or struggling with a fierce, implacable enemy. The life of a Christian man or woman is the life of a spiritual warrior. (Webber, 2001, p. 11)

The Word of Knowledge – "The word of knowledge is the supernatural revelation by the Holy Ghost of certain facts in the mind of God." (Hagin, 1991, p 75)

<u>Contact Information</u>

Apostle Dr. Ernest Maddox
Dr. Ernest Maddox Ministries

Address
P.O. Box 48547, Oak Park, MI. 48237
Phone 248-796-8523

Email: drddox@yahoo.com
Email: dr.ernest.maddox@gmail.com
Website: www.dremaddox.org

Short Biography

Dr. Maddox has served God for over forty four years and has been a leader in the areas of Youth Ministry, Radio Ministry, Leadership Training Ministry, Satellite/TV Ministry (Total Christian Television), and Inner Healing-Prayer and Deliverance Ministry. Dr. Maddox has served as a Deacon, Minister, and Elder. Dr. Maddox is currently the Pastor of the P.O.I.N.T.E. of Light Christian Center, which Jesus Christ led him to establish. Dr. Maddox is known nationally as a trainer, motivational speaker, and man of God in religious and secular arenas. Dr. Maddox is also President of Dr. E. Maddox Ministries. Dr. Maddox was called to be an Apostle by Jesus Christ, and this was confirmed by three men who are also Apostles.

Dr. Maddox has seen the power of God to save and deliver. God called him from a life of gang banging and drug dealing, to a life focused on helping others. God took a young man, with little more than a sixth grade education, and led him through a process from GED to Ph.D., and beyond. Dr. Maddox has earned these degrees, Bachelor of Science, Master of Arts/Business, Master of Public Administration, Doctor of Philosophy, Doctor of Ministry and Doctor of Education. Dr. Maddox has served as Dean of the Graduate Schools of Mission Leadership and Pastoral Leadership, at Destiny University in Ghana, Africa, and also served as an instructor at Power of the Word Bible College in Detroit, MI. Dr. Maddox has served and taught the word of God in South Africa and Nigeria.

Dr. Maddox began his walk relative to Inner Healing and Deliverance Ministry over forty four years ago. He was involved in a very conservative church organization from 1969 until 2000. What Jesus Christ was revealing to him was viewed as taboo in that environment. As a result Dr. Maddox had to rely on God the Father, Jesus Christ, the Holy Spirit and his wife, Barbara, of over thirty seven years. Dr. Maddox has been led to share some revelations in this book, "Impact of A Deliverance Prayer", (A Study of Deliverance Ministry). Dr. Maddox has consulted with Dr. Ed Murphy, "The Handbook For Spiritual Warfare", Dr. L. David Mitchell, "Liberty In Jesus" Apostle Gene B. Moody, "Deliverance Manual" and Apostle Fred Harris, Church of the Risen Christ - Inner Healing & Deliverance Ministry.

Dr. Maddox is available for consulting, training, teaching and preaching in all areas of ministry. See contact information on the preceding page. Thank you for purchasing this book. This act will aid the work of Jesus Christ and help bring the message of Inner Healing and Deliverance to the world.

"His Kingdom Come; Amen"

www.ingramcontent.com/pod-product-compliance
Lightning Source LLC
LaVergne TN
LVHW051626080426
835511LV00016B/2196